From the exhibition held in the galleries of
the Society of Illustrators Museum of
American Illustration
128 East 63rd Street, New York, NY 10021
February 4-April 15, 1987

SOCIETY OF ILLUSTRATORS, INC.
128 EAST 63RD STREET, NEW YORK, NY 10021

ISBN 08230-4886-1
Library of Congress Catalog Card Number 59-10849

*Distributors to the trade in the United States
and Canada:*

Watson-Guptill Publications
1515 Broadway, New York, NY 10036

Distributed throughout the rest of the world by:
Hearst Publications International
105 Madison Avenue, New York, NY 10016

Publisher:
Madison Square Press
10 East 23rd Street, New York, NY 10010

Editor: Arpi Ermoyan   *Designer:* Robert Anthony

Printed in Japan

Photo Credits: Award Winners/Peter de Seve by
Susan Rubins; Lane Smith by Molly Leach. Jurors/
Wendell Minor by George Kanatous; Rudolph Hog-
lund by Tony Suarez. Hall of Fame, Maurice
Sendak, Illustrators 29 Committees, Awards Pre-
sentation/by George Kanatous.

THE SOCIETY OF ILLUSTRATORS 29th ANNUAL OF AMERICAN ILLUSTRATION

ILLUSTRATORS 29

1/29

Published for the Society of Illustrators by Madison Square Press, Inc., New York

TABLE OF CONTENTS

PRESIDENT'S MESSAGE

PORTRAIT BY HODGES SOILEAU

As the kudos for *Illustrators 29* reach our offices in ever-increasing numbers, I wish to join in the praise expressed to those who comprise the various committees and who carry the heavy burden of its responsibility. Untiring efforts and long hours are the norm for all who have been associated with '29'. Once again we have produced a distinctive volume of which we are very proud.

As the number of entries for the annual show grows from year to year, the juries have the increasingly difficult task of carefully selecting a small fraction of the best in illustration out of some 8,000 excellent entries. These are shown in two concurrent segments at the Society of Illustrators: the first half of the show consists of the Editorial and Book categories; the second part features the Advertising and Institutional categories.

All accepted entries become part of and are featured in our yearly volume of The Society of Illustrators Annual of American Illustration.

I urge everyone, if you have not already done so, to start collecting these volumes—soon to be collectors' items. These books offer a tremendous insight into illustration, an 'art form' gaining strength and world attention for the past 100 years.

I would like to salute all illustrators who, because of their excellent entries, were included in the Illustrators 29 Exhibition and subsequently, this 29th Annual Book. Rather than single out individual talent responsible for the excellent production of this volume, I would like to thank the publisher, Madison Square Press, and everyone associated with it.

Walter Hortens

Walter Hortens
President, Society of Illustrators, 1985-1987

AWARDS PRESENTATION

Because of the growing response for tickets to the Annual Exhibition Awards Presentations, the Past Chairmen's Committee decided it was high time to move this event from the Society's headquarters to larger facilities.

Thanks to Chairman Jim Sharpe and his committee, the stunning Tower Suite atop the Time-Life Building was secured for the evening's festivities. Following delicious hors d'oeuvres and plentiful libation came the presentation of Gold and Silver Medals to the award-winning artists and art directors.

Acting as MC was Geoffrey Moss, with SI President Walter Hortens and Jim Sharpe handing out the awards. Terry Brown read descriptions of the evolution of the award-winning pieces. Throughout the evening selections from the Illustrators 29 Exhibition were projected on two screens. It was a glamorous evening indeed, capped off by music and dancing.

Congratulations to the award winners, the Chairman, and all who helped make this the Society's "main event" of the year!

Wendell Minor, John Craft, Hamilton King Award Winner Kinuko Craft and Marshall Arisman

Society Director Terry Brown, Brad Holland and Judy Pedersen

President Walter Hortens and Chairman Jim Sharpe

Award winners Joe Saffold, Richard Whitney and Braldt Bralds

CHAIRMAN'S MESSAGE

As Chairman of Illustrators 29, it is *truly* a pleasure for me to congratulate all of you selected for this show. Your art now becomes a part of history in this book. To have your artwork selected by your peers, from nearly 8,000 entries from throughout the country, is not a small accomplishment. Survey this book closely and examine what you and your contemporaries have created. It is very, very good! Take a moment to give yourself a pat (or two) on the back, to be proud of yourself...then take a deep breath, and get back to work. Try not to sit for too long on your laurels. This book *is* history now...exciting, beautiful, and imaginative...but history! The clock has already started ticking on Illustrators 30, 31, 32, and so on. Next year's heroes have already done their sketches and are moving to the finish. Illustration moves at a fast pace...like a deadline—it waits for no one. That is as it should be.

What a nifty challenge this business is—it's all out there for someone—anyone—ever changing! If you're just out of art school or a street-wise 15-year vet...the challenge is there for you—*you can make a difference*. You can contribute, you can influence, either somewhat or greatly, to the course of illustration with your own imagination and creativity. It's not easy... it takes perseverance, it takes patience, it takes a lot of heart...and of course, it demands a lot of sweat and tears and plain ol' hard work. But the opportunity is always there for anyone...anytime! Illustration is a tough, demanding little business, but every year someone does come along and makes a special difference...

...next year could be *your* year...

...or maybe the next?

Jim Sharpe
Chairman, Illustrators 29

ILLUSTRATORS 29 ANNUAL EXHIBITION

Chairman/Jim Sharpe
Assistant Chairman/Chris Spollen
Poster Designer/John deCesare
Poster Artist/Hodges Soileau
Hanging Chairmen/Tim Raglin,
Bill Purdom
SI Staff/Terrence Brown, Director,
James Capizutto, Cathy Citarella,
Mary Citarella, Anna Lee Fuchs,
Ellise Fuchs, Phyllis Harvey, Norma Pimsler,
Frederic Taraba

ILLUSTRATORS 29 ANNUAL BOOK

Editor/Arpi Ermoyan
Designer/Robert Anthony
Production & Advertising/Janet Weithas

SI Staff, left to right, front row: Phyllis Harvey, Terrence Brown, Norma Pimsler; back row: Ellise Fuchs, Cathy Citarella, Fred Taraba, Anna Lee Fuchs

Jim Sharpe, Chairman; Chris Spollen, Associate Chairman

Left to right: Arpi Ermoyan, Editor; Bob Anthony, Designer; Janet Weithas, Production and Advertising

John deCesare, Poster Designer; Hodges Soileau, Poster Artist

iv

JURYING THE ANNUAL EXHIBITION: HOW IT WORKS

The most important function of the Annual Exhibition Past Chairmen's Committee is the selection of jurors which takes place approximately seven months prior to the actual jurying.

A large blackboard is set up with five vertical columns—four for the categories (Advertising, Editorial, Book & Institutional) and one in which to list diverse types of jurors. Every effort is made to create a good mix of illustrators and art directors with a wide range of tastes.

The first jurors selected are four Society of Illustrator members, each of whom acts as chairman of one of the categories. Eight additional jurors, including non-Society members, are then selected for each category. In order to avoid bias, jurors are placed in categories other than those from which their primary income is derived professionally. A period of three years must elapse before a juror may serve again. Jurors may not win awards in the category they are judging.

Jurying takes place during four days in October—one category each day. All published entries are set out in piles of black-and-white, 2-color, full color, and are also broken down according to size within that framework. After the jurors have completed viewing all the entries and have marked those which they feel qualify for the show, the staff sorts them into groups of 'like' votes and those with the highest are brought back to be considered for awards.

During the initial voting, jurors are asked to vote silently, without discussion, but when the selection of awards gets underway, jurors are free to express their views on why they think a certain piece merits an award.

The unpublished entries, submitted in slide form, are projected on a screen and voted on by means of a unique voting machine which enables each juror to cast his vote privately. Awards for unpublished pieces are selected the following week by the Balancing Jury.

The Balancing Jury is composed of the current Exhibition Chairman, the four Category Chairmen, and two Past Chairmen. Since each artist accepted in the show is allowed no more than three pieces in a category and no more than five in the entire show (not counting award-winning pieces), it is the Balancing Jury's responsibility to whittle down those exceeding this number.

The Society of Illustrators takes great pride in the integrity with which this show has been run over the years and intends to maintain this high standard.

ANNUAL SHOW CHAIRMEN

'59 DAVID K. STONE
'60 HARRY CARTER
'61 LEN JOSSEL
'62 AL MUENCHEN
'63 GEORGE SAMERJAN
'64 DON MOSS
'65 JERRY McDANIEL
'66 GERALD McCONNELL
'67 SHANNON STIRNWEIS
10 HARRY SCHAARE
11 CHUCK McVICKER
12 ALVIN PIMSLER
13 MARBURY BROWN
14 AL PISANO
15 JAMES CROWELL
16 BOB CUEVAS
17 ROLAND DESCOMBES
18 WARREN ROGERS
19 HOWARD KOSLOW
20 DOUG JOHNSON
21 EILEEN HEDY SCHULTZ
22 SANDY HUFFAKER
23 BERNIE KARLIN
24 PAST CHAIRMEN'S COMMITTEE
25 PAST CHAIRMEN'S COMMITTEE
26 ROLAND DESCOMBES
27 BARNEY PLOTKIN
28 JOHN WITT
29 JIM SHARPE

Society of Illustrators

HALL OF FAME

for distinguished achievement in the

Art of Illustration

THE SOCIETY OF ILLUSTRATORS HALL OF FAME

Each year the Society of Illustrators elects to its Hall of Fame those artists who have made an outstanding contribution to the art of illustration throughout the years.

The list of previous winners is truly a 'Who's Who' of illustration. Former presidents of the Society meet annually to elect those who will be so honored.

At a formal dinner in June of 1987 the Hall of Fame Award was presented to Maurice Sendak, and Haddon Sundblom was honored posthumously. A short biography of each man and examples of their work are presented in the following pages.

HALL OF FAME COMMITTEE

Willis Pyle/Chairman
Past Presidents of the Society:
Walter Brooks, Harry Carter,
Stevan Dohanos, Tran Mawicke,
Charles McVicker, John A. Moodie,
Howard Munce, Alvin J. Pimsler,
Warren Rogers, William Schneider,
Shannon Stirnweis, David K. Stone,
John Witt, D. L. Cramer

1987 HALL OF FAME

Maurice Sendak
Haddon Sundblom*

PREVIOUS HALL OF FAME

Norman Rockwell 1958
Dean Cornwell 1959
Harold Von Schmidt 1959
Fred Cooper 1960
Floyd Davis 1961
Edward Wilson 1962
Walter Biggs 1963
Arthur William Brown 1964
Al Parker 1965
Al Dorne 1966
Robert Fawcett 1967
Peter Helck 1968
Austin Briggs 1969
Rube Goldberg 1970
Stevan Dohanos 1971
Ray Prohaska 1972
Jon Whitcomb 1973
Tom Lovell 1974
Charles Dana Gibson* 1974
N.C. Wyeth* 1974
Bernie Fuchs 1975
Maxfield Parrish* 1975
Howard Pyle* 1975
John Falter 1976
Winslow Homer* 1976
Harvey Dunn* 1976
Robert Peak 1977
Wallace Morgan* 1977
J.C. Leyendecker* 1977
Coby Whitmore 1978
Norman Price* 1978
Frederic Remington* 1978
Ben Stahl 1979
Edwin Austin Abbey* 1979
Lorraine Fox* 1979
Saul Tepper 1980
Howard Chandler Christy* 1980
James Montgomery Flagg* 1980
Stan Galli 1981
Frederic R. Gruger* 1981
John Gannam* 1981
John Clymer 1982
Henry P. Raleigh* 1982
Eric (Carl Erickson)* 1982
Mark English 1983
Noel Sickles* 1983
Franklin Booth* 1983
Neysa Moran McMein* 1984
John LaGatta* 1984
James Williamson* 1984
Robert Weaver 1985
Charles Marion Russell* 1985
Arthur Burdett Frost* 1985
Al Hirschfeld 1986
Rockwell Kent* 1986

*Presented posthumously

HALL OF FAME 1987
MAURICE SENDAK (b. 1928)

Maurice Sendak was born in 1928 and grew up in Brooklyn, New York. His father was a successful dressmaker in Manhattan. He had two older siblings, Natalie and Jack. The family moved often, but each new address brought a new window through which the young Maurice viewed the world. It was the excitement of the street life he saw that fascinated him: the complexities of human relations, the character studies, and the exposure of emotions. He stored all of these images away as fodder for future storytelling.

After attending Lafayette High School, he studied at the Art Students League under John Groth, who instilled in him a sense of the fun in illustration. He soon landed a position doing window display at F.A.O. Schwartz, the famous toy store. This proved to be a fortunate break as it was there that he was introduced to Ursula Nordstrom, an editor at Harper & Brothers. At the age of 22, he was given his first children's book commission. When *The Wonderful Farm* by Marcel Ayme was published Sendak entered the ranks of professional children's book illustrators.

From 1951 to 1962, Sendak illustrated over 50 books: *A Hole is to Dig*, *A Simple Concept Book*, *Charlotte and the White Horse* (his first in full color), *Little Bears* (the first in a series with the dual outlook of nature and humanity), *The Nutshell Library* (a series of four books, small in size, which were immensely popular), *Kenny's Window* (the first that he also wrote), and *Nikolenka's Childhood* (which featured a full text).

With the publication of *Where the Wild Things Are* in 1963, Sendak's career took a quantum leap. The book received the Caldecott Award from the American Librarian's Association. It also received some chiding reviews from those who felt the images were too frightful for the young. Sendak saw it as the young hero's journey through frustration and anger to a cathartic taming of 'the wild things.' This is a picture book in which the words and illustrations are interdependent.

The '60s were an important decade of growth and development for Sendak. If they had punctuation marks, one surely was the heart attack he suffered in England in 1967. His works

Geoffrey Moss, MC; Maurice Sendak

shortly thereafter, including the final Little Bear book, showed a more somber tone. Another notable event that year was the death of Jennie, Sendak's sealyham dog, a devoted friend. *Higgelty, Piggelty Pop* was published shortly thereafter and is a tribute to his dog.

The Night Kitchen was to be Sendak's next blockbuster and second Caldecott. Again, the story is a dream/fantasy with a young hero falling through space, facing dread and terror. After overcoming difficult circumstances, he returns home to the safety of his bed. This book has a decidedly 1930's flair, a mixture of Busby Berkeley, Laurel and Hardy, and Mickey Mouse.

To any children's book illustrator, the works of the Brothers Grimm have to rank as the ultimate assignment. These tales, which at the time were published in order to save oral folklore which was being lost, are written in a matter-of-fact manner, which Sendak feels children appreciate.

The Grimm tales were a major endeavor which lasted over 15 months. As usual, he worked on nothing else at the same time. He travelled to Germany and Wales to get a feel for the settings, researched the many previous editions, and even purchased an original 1819 edition. After 15 months he was done—exhausted —but done. These illustrations are small, even claustrophobic. They mirror the deep psychological tales that the Grimms were telling. However, they fire the imagination and are among his best illustrations in terms of design, concept, and drawing.

In the mid-'70s he branched out into a different media: a half-hour version of his Really Rosie stories aired in 1975, with music by Carole King. A note on Rosie: she was one of those sidewalk specials whom Sendak watched from his Brooklyn window. She wove tales, was wise beyond her young years and intrigued him. Like

Jennie, the dog, Rosie appears from time to time in many of his works.

In 1979, *Outside Over There* was published, which proved to be as important as *Wild Things* and *Night Kitchen*. Once again, it is a fantasy, a simple story. Goblins steal baby, hero works out his problems while rescuing the baby; but it took over 100 drafts of text before being finalized.

His more recent works include stage settings and animated videos; all in all an active career with a definite direction: to expose the child in all of us, to help exercise the muscle of imagination, and to provide a forum for young people in which to work out their deepest fears and angers. Those lofty goals have been achieved by Maurice Sendak over and over throughout the years.

Terrence Brown
Director, Society of Illustrators

Detail from Where the Wild Things Are, 1963
© *1963 by Maurice Sendak*

Half-title page from In the Night Kitchen, 1970
© *1970 by Maurice Sendak*

From In the Night Kitchen, 1970
© *1970 by Maurice Sendak*

From In the Night Kitchen, 1970
© *1970 by Maurice Sendak*

HALL OF FAME 1987
HADDON HUBBARD SUNDBLOM
(1899-1976)

Charcoal portrait by James Montgomery Flagg

*'So Unaware of You,' illustration for Cream of Wheat Cereal, 1928
Collection of Nabisco Brands Inc.*

Haddon Hubbard Sundblom was a dominant force in American advertising illustration, through his own work and through that of his studio, Stevens Sundblom & Henry. Established in Chicago in the mid-1920s when that city was the center of advertising in the country, he and his studio produced a brilliant series of paintings for an extraordinary number of major accounts, including Coca-Cola, Cashmere Bouquet, Procter & Gamble, Packard, Buick, Pierce Arrow, Ford, Frigidaire, Kelvinator, Westinghouse, Mazda Lamps, Quaker Oats, Pet Milk, Goodyear, Gulf Oil, Maxwell House Coffee, Cream of Wheat, Kellogg's, United Brewers Foundation, Lucky Strike, and many others.

The Studio was also a valuable training ground for many top illustrators, including Harry Anderson, Earl Blossom, Al Buell, Matt Clark, Gil Elvgren, Nick Hufford, Charles Kinghan, Al Kortner, Al Moore, Herb Olsen, Walter Richards, James Schucker, Euclid Shook, Bob Skemp, Thornton Utz, and Coby Whitmore. Sundblom himself greatly admired and was greatly influenced by Anders Zorn, J.C. Leyendecker (to whom he owed a debt for his Coca-Cola Santa Claus), John Singer Sargent, Robert Henri, and Sorolla; he amalgamated their techniques into his own dashing, a la prima style.

His accomplishments were especially impressive for having had to quit school at thirteen. He was born in Muskegon, Michigan, the ninth child of a Finnish shipbuilder turned carpenter. The family was poor; with so many children and only seasonal employment available, it was hard to make ends meet. When Haddon's mother died, he had to leave school to earn his own keep. For years he worked for construction firms during the day and at night attended high school art classes; later he studied at the Chicago Art Institute and the American Academy of Art.

On the strength of his school samples, he was finally taken on as an apprentice at the Charles Everett Johnson Studio in 1920 for the promised sum of $15 a week. After five weeks of running errands, he wondered why he wasn't being paid and found out that his name had not even been entered on the payroll. He had to settle for $10 a week to be signed on and paid. Another duty was to clean brushes for luminaries like McClelland Barclay, Andrew Loomis, Frank Snapp, Harry Timmins, Will Foster, and Roy Spreter. He quickly learned his craft by watching them work and was soon able to start his own career. One of his earliest assignments was to create a symbol for Quaker Oats, still in use with only minor changes after over sixty years.

In 1925, together with Howard Stevens and Edwin Henry, he started the studio that was to quickly build a reputation as the biggest and best, employing thirty artists and occupying a whole floor in the Palmolive Building. It was an irreverent, argumentative, and very talented crew with good cross fertilization of ideas. But should a question arise, Sundblom could win any argument, simply by proving it with his brush.

Although usually too busy to take on editorial illustration assignments, Sundblom did a few covers for *Woman's Home Companion* and the *Ladies' Home Journal*, as well as some fiction illustration for them and for *Cosmopolitan* and *Good Housekeeping* magazines. They were always outstanding and make us wish he had done more.

One of the first accounts Sundblom landed for his new studio was Coca-Cola. He quickly

made some rough sketches for their agency in an emergency. They liked his work so much that he kept the account from then on. In 1931, wishing to thank the public for supporting their product, Coca-Cola asked him to create a Santa Claus accompanied only by the line: 'The Pause that Refreshes.' He continued painting Santa annually for the next thirty years, at first using a retired salesman as the model, but as time went on he himself aged into the perfect model for Santa.

Although best remembered for his Coca-Cola campaign and especially the annual Santa Claus, all of his work exemplified his sunny spirit. His were brightly colored, idealized and cheerful images that conveyed the same upbeat feeling about the products he illustrated and made him such a favorite with advertisers and the public alike.

Walt Reed
Illustration Historian

'Never Say Die,' Ladies' Home Journal, August, 1938,
collection of the Society of Illustrators Museum of American Illustration

Coca-Cola advertisement.

HAMILTON KING AWARD

The Hamilton King Award is presented annually for the finest illustration in the Annual Exhibition by a member of the Society of Illustrators. The selection is made by former recipients of this award. The 1987 winner is Kinuko Craft for her painting of Queen Elizabeth done for ITT.

HAMILTON KING AWARD WINNERS

Paul Calle 1965
Bernie Fuchs 1966
Mark English 1967
Robert Peak 1968
Alan Cober 1969
Ray Ameijide 1970
Miriam Schottland 1971
Charles Santore 1972
Dave Blossom 1973
Fred Otnes 1974
Carol Anthony 1975
Judith Jampel 1976
Leo & Diane Dillon 1977
Daniel Schwartz 1978
William Teason 1979
Wilson McLean 1980
Gerald McConnell 1981
Robert Heindel 1982
Robert M. Cunningham 1983
Braldt Bralds 1984
Attila Hejja 1985
Doug Johnson 1986
Kinuko Y. Craft 1987

HAMILTON KING AWARD 1987
KINUKO Y. CRAFT

Named 'silk-child' by her maternal grandfather, Kinuko Craft grew up in a small village in Japan, surrounded by nature. 'My grandfather was an art collector and my nursery books were art books of the collections of the world's museums. I told myself stories about the pictures. Grandfather had a Maxfield Parrish print, a painting of dreams and the romantic. I think I am a romantic.'

After graduating from the Municipal College of Fine and Industrial Art in Kanazawa, the Japanese sister city of Buffalo, Craft requested sponsorship from various design studios to enter the United States. She received a favorable response from one Chicago studio and, without knowing a word of English, arrived in America in 1964. Soon she was enrolled at the Art Institute of Chicago, thinking it was the Illinois Institute of Technology's design school which she had heard of in Japan. Though she discovered her error, she remained at the Art Institute because by then she was convinced she would become an illustrator. For the year-and-a-half she attended school, Craft benefited most from the Institute's collection which greatly impressed her.

'Sick of school,' Craft began working in Chicago's illustration studios until she hired a representative and launched her freelance career.

Playboy magazine gave her the break into editorial illustration which helped her get other work from top magazines such as *Time*, *Forbes*, *National Geographic*, *Newsweek*, *Cosmopolitan*, *National Lampoon*, and *Oui*.

Over the years Craft's range of clients has continually expanded to include major advertising and packaging clients such as ITT, AT&T, Clairol and Celestial Seasonings Teas while her work continues to be seen on major magazine covers and book jackets.

About her illustration assignments, Craft says: 'Since I am telling the visual side of the story, I must create an atmosphere that fits the flavor of the story. When I'm assigned a historic subject I research for costume and environment, but mainly search for the style of the artists who existed at the period and try to paint with their procedures.' Because of her insatiable curiosity about art history, as well as other subjects including archeology, her reference library is immense: 'I used to use the public library picture files, but now they are a disaster, so I buy books. Books are my best friends.'

With the reference available for assignments which range from space-age themes to pre-Raphaelite atmospheres, Craft is ready to tackle any illustration problem. However, she says, 'It may have taken the artist of the Renaissance period three or six months to make a painting, but I have to do the assignment in a couple of weeks.'

After diligent research, she gets her mind working the way artists of a particular period worked. Then, 'when I am ready to paint, it is as if I am living in that time. It is exactly like an actor doing a part. As when an actor has to portray a really violent person, I have to condition myself to do a violent painting.'

In 1983 Craft exhibited her work at the Society of Illustrators in a one-woman show. In the Illustrators 29 Annual Show she received the Gold Medal in the advertising category for the portrait of Queen Elizabeth which was also chosen for the Hamilton King Award.

She and her husband reside in Connecticut where twelve-hour work days are standard, often including weekends. She sleeps little and loves to work. Of her art she says, 'It is the only thing I have, I just can't do anything else.'

'All my possessions for a moment of time.' Portrait of Queen Elizabeth I for ITT.

Diane Dillon
Chairman
Illustrator

Wendell Minor
Illustrator

Mark A. Fredrickson
Gold Medal

David Bartels
Art Director, Bartels & Co.

Andrea Mistretta
Illustrator

Peter De Sève
Silver Medal

Chris Blossom
Illustrator

Rafal Olbinski
Illustrator

Lane Smith
Silver Medal

Joe Ciardiello
Illustrator

Joseph Stelmach
Art Director, RCA Records

Greg Spalenka
Silver Medal

Mark Hess
Illustrator

EDITORIAL

28

1 Artist: **MARK A. FREDRICKSON**   Art Director: Mark A. Fredrickson   Magazine: Arizona Daily Star

GOLD MEDAL

2 Artist: **PETER DE SÈVE**   Art Director: Ken Kendrick   Magazine: The New York Times

SILVER MEDAL

3 Artist: **LANE SMITH**   Art Director: Joan Ferrell   Magazine: Travel and Leisure

SILVER MEDAL

4 Artist: **GREG SPALENKA**   Art Directors: Tom Staebler / Kerig Pope   Magazine: Playboy

SILVER MEDAL

5 Artist: **JAMES McMULLAN**   Art Director: Carol Carson   Magazine: Scholastic, Inc.

6
Artist: **ELWOOD SMITH**
Art Director: Rip Georges
Magazine: L.A. Style

7 Artist: **BO STERK**

8
Artist: **GEOFFREY MOSS**
Art Director: Barrie Stern
Magazine: Venture

9 Artist: **JOSEPH DANIEL FIEDLER**

10 Artist: **BRALDT BRALDS** Art Director: Kerig Pope Magazine: Playboy

11 Artist: **MALCOLM T. LIEPKE** Art Director: Richard Warner Magazine: Sports Illustrated

12
Artist: **PAULO PIGLIA**
Art Director: Richard Warner
Magazine: Sports Illustrated

13
Artist: **MARSHALL ARISMAN**
Art Director: Walter Herdeg
Magazine: Graphis

14
Artist: **SIMMS TABACK**
Art Director: Carol Carson
Magazine: Let's Find Out

15
Artist: **J.P. SCHMELZER**
Art Director: Ben Yonzon
Client: Chicago Tribune Tempo

16 Artist: **B. JOHANSEN NEWMAN** Art Director: Lisa Sergi Magazine: Ultrasport

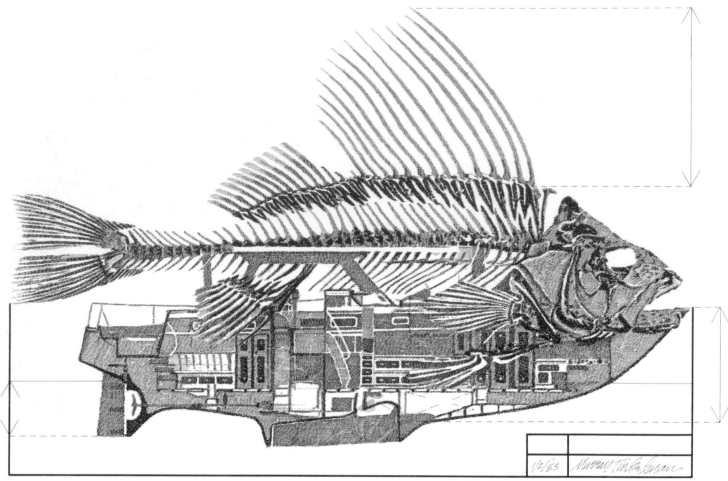

17 Artist: **MURRAY TINKELMAN** Art Director: Bob Farber Client: U & lc

18 Artist: **KAREL HAVLICEK** Art Director: J. Robert Teringo Magazine: National Geographic

19
Artist: **ALEXANDER HUNTER**
Art Director: Jane Palecek
Magazine: The Washington Times

20 Artist: **HODGES SOILEAU** Art Director: Mindy Stanton Magazine: Field and Stream

22
Artist: **BOB CONGE**
Art Director: Carla Block
Magazine: Art Direction

23
Artist: **DEBORAH HEALY**
Art Director: Jerry Sealy
Magazine: The Plain Dealer

21
Artist: **JOYCE KITCHELL**
Art Director: James Lawrence
Magazine: Harrowsmith

24 Artist: **ROBERT CRAWFORD** Art Director: Wendy Reingold Magazine: World Tennis

25
Artist: **RICHARD SPARKS**
Art Director: Richard Warner
Magazine: Sports Illustrated

26
Artist: **LARRY CARROLL**
Art Director: Christopher Sloan
Magazine: Financial Executive

27
Artist: **LARRY RIVERS**
Art Director: Richard Warner
Magazine: Sports Illustrated

28
Artist: **BRIAN AJHAR**
Art Director: Randy Dunbar
Magazine: Daily News Magazine

29 Artist: **GREG SPALENKA**   Art Directors: Richard Warner / Larry Gendron   Magazine: Sports Illustrated

30
Artist: **QUANG HO**
Art Director: Richard Deolivera
Magazine: The International

31 Artist: **BART GOLDMAN**   Art Director: Lisa Orsini   Magazine: Macuser

32 Artist: **DAVID BECK** Art Directors: Dan Jursa / Judie Anderson Magazine: Chicago Tribune

33 Artist: **MAX GINSBURG** Art Director: Robert Best Magazine: New York

34
Artist: **KENT WILLIAMS**
Art Director: Mary Zisk
Magazine: PC

35
Artist: **BRAD HOLLAND**
Art Director: Wayne Fitzpatrick
Magazine: Science '85

36 Artist: **ALAN E. COBER**   Art Director: Wanda Yueh   Magazine: Video

37 Artist: **DEBRA WHITE** Art Director: Audrey Razgaitis Magazine: The New York Times

38
Artist: **THOMAS WOODRUFF**
Art Director: Mike Marcum
Magazine: Campus Voice

40
Artist: **JOSE CRUZ**
Art Director: Derek Ungless
Magazine: Rolling Stone

41
Artist: **KENT WILLIAMS**
Art Director: Hans Teensma
Magazine: New England Monthly

42
Artist: **ROBERT GANTT STEELE**

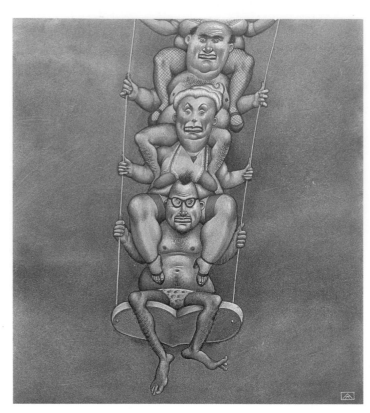

43
Artist: **ANITA KUNZ**
Art Director: Kent Barton
Magazine: Sunshine

44
Artist: **JEFFREY J. SMITH**
Art Director: Fabian Baron
Magazine: Gentleman's Quarterly

45
Artist: **ENID HATTON**
Art Director: Tina Adamek
Magazine: Postgraduate Medicine

46 Artist: **NANCY STAHL** Art Director: Arlene Lappen Magazine: Working Woman

47
Artist: **DOUGLAS FRASER**
Art Director: Wendell K. Harrington
Magazine: Esquire

48
Artist: **DOUGLAS FRASER**
Art Director: Malcolm Frouman
Magazine: Business Week

49 Artist: **MEL ODOM** Art Directors: Tom Staebler / Kerig Pope Magazine: Playboy

50
Artist: **VIVIENNE FLESHER**
Art Director: Lynn Staley
Magazine: The Boston Globe

51
Artist: **VIVIENNE FLESHER**
Art Director: Ronn Campisi
Magazine: The Boston Globe

52
Artist: **JOANIE SCHWARZ**
Art Director: Richard Bleiweiss
Magazine: Penthouse

53
Artist: **JAMES McMULLAN**
Art Director: Bob Ciano
Magazine: Life

54
Artist: **MALCOLM T. LIEPKE**

55
Artist: **BURT SILVERMAN**
Art Director: Rudy Hoglund
Magazine: Time

56
Artist: **MALCOLM T. LIEPKE**
Art Director: Richard Warner
Magazine: Sports Illustrated

57 Artist: **EDWARD SOREL** Art Director: Judy Garlan Magazine: Atlantic Monthly

58
Artist: **MICHAEL PARASKEVAS**
Art Director: Marshall Arisman
Magazine: Print

COALE

59
Artist: **HOWARD COALE**
Art Director: Paul Davis
Magazine: Normal

COALE

60
Artist: **HOWARD COALE**
Art Director: Paul Davis
Magazine: Normal

61
Artist: **KEN WESTPHAL**
Art Director: Ken Westphal
Client: KANU FM 91.5

62 Artist: **QUANG HO** Art Director: Bob Fuller Magazine: Discipleship Journal

63 Artist: **DOUGLAS SMITH** Art Director: Lynn Staley Magazine: The Boston Globe

64
Artist: **MARY S. FLOCK**
Art Director: Mick Cochran
Magazine: Providence Journal-Bulletin

65
Artist: **CATHIE BLECK**
Art Director: Fred Woodward
Magazine: Texas Monthly

66
Artist: **MARK PENBERTHY**
Art Directors: Michael Walsh / Al Brandtner
Magazine: Michigan

67
Artist: **BOB NEWMAN**
Art Director: Miriam Smith
Magazine: Newsday

68 Artist: **ALAN REINGOLD** Art Director: Richard Bleiweiss Magazine: Penthouse

69
Artist: **KENT WILLIAMS**
Art Director: Mary Zisk
Magazine: PC

70 Artist: **CARY HENRIE**   Art Director: Joe Connolly   Magazine: Boy's Life

71
Artist: **LARS W. JUSTINEN**
Art Directors: Ed Guthero / Lars Justinen
Magazine: Signs of the Times

72 Artist: **BART GOLDMAN**   Art Director: Sara Christensen   Magazine: Best of Business Quarterly

73
Artist: **GREG SPALENKA**
Art Director: John Iselly
Magazine: Science '86

74
Artist: **STEPHEN T. JOHNSON**

75
Artist: **KUNIO HAGIO**
Art Director: Richard Bleiweiss
Magazine: Penthouse

76
Artist: **GARY VISKUPIC**
Art Director: Miriam Smith
Magazine: Newsday

77
Artist: **JEFFREY J. SMITH**
Art Director: Linda Evans
Magazine: New Marriage

78
Artist: **DAVID SHANNON**
Art Director: Janet Froelich
Magazine: Daily News Magazine

79 Artist: **ETIENNE DELESSERT**   Art Director: Judy Garlan   Magazine: Atlantic Monthly

80 Artist: **JOHN THOMPSON** Art Director: Victor J. Closi Magazine: Field and Stream

81
Artist: **MICHAEL GARLAND**
Art Director: Alice Degenhardt
Magazine: Creative Living

8
Artist: **GORDON SWENARTO**
Art Director: William Kuh
Magazine: Medical Economics for Surgeon

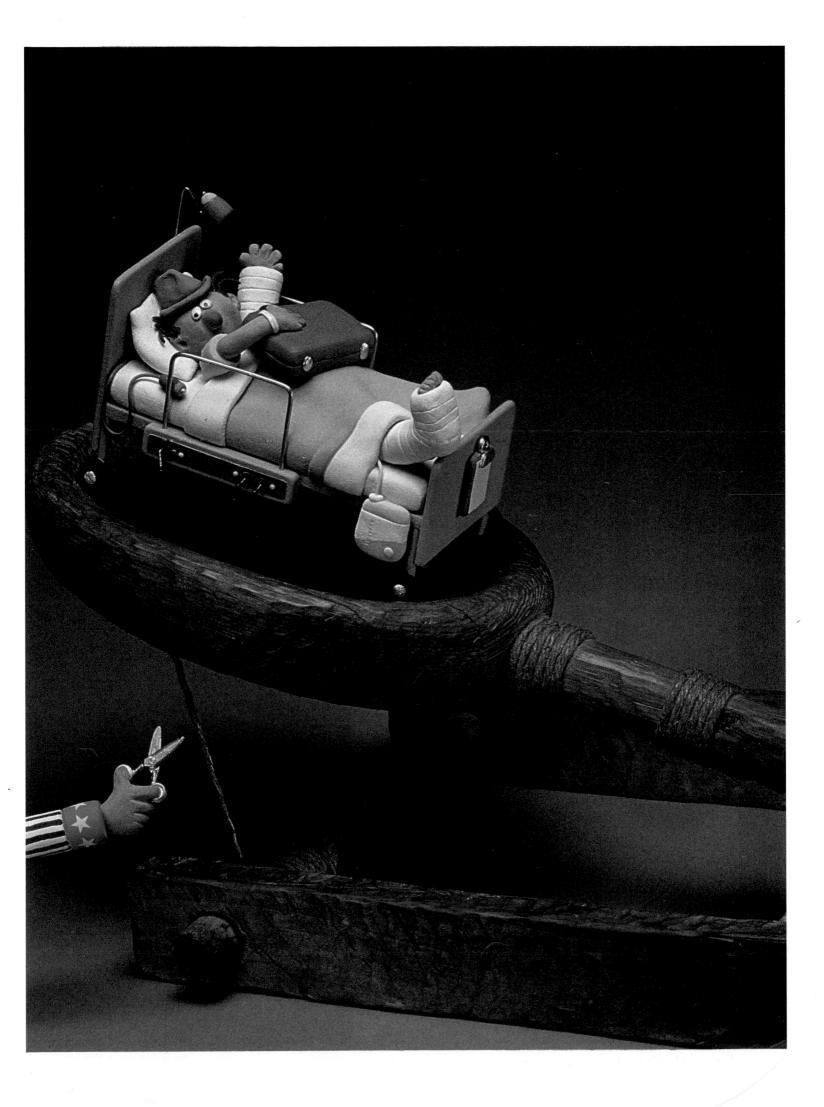

83 Artist: **EARL KELENY** Art Director: Anne Dillon Magazine: Run

84
Artist: **CARY HENRIE**
Art Director: Lisa Orsini
Magazine: Macuser

85
Artist: **BRIAN AJHAR**
Art Director: Ellen Blissman
Magazine: Money

86
Artist: **ROB DAY**
Art Director: Michael Bilicki
Magazine: Florida Trend

87
Artist: **BRIAN AJHAR**
Art Director: Gary Bernloehr
Magazine: Georgia Trend

88
Artist: **GUY BILLOUT**
Art Director: Margery Peters
Magazine: Fortune

89
Artist: **CHRIS McALLISTER**
Art Director: Chris McAllister
Magazine: Administrative Radiology

90
Artist: **GEOFFREY MOSS**
Art Director: Gary Bernloehr
Magazine: Georgia Trend

91
Artist: **DANIEL MAFFIA**
Art Directors: Arlene Lappen / Gail Tauber
Magazine: Working Woman

92 Artist: **RAFAL OLBINSKI** Art Director: Ron Myerson Magazine: Newsweek International

93
Artist: **BOB CONGE**
Art Director: Riki Allred
Magazine: Northeast

94 Artist: **BART GOLDMAN** Art Director: Audrey Razgaitis Magazine: The New York Times

95
Artist: **STEVE JOHNSON**
Art Director: Judy Sell
Magazine: Minneapolis Star and Tribune

96
Artist: **JOHN MAZZINI**
Art Director: Michael Pardo
Magazine: Automobile Quarterly

97 Artist: **GUY BILLOUT** Art Director: Judy Garlan Magazine: Atlantic Monthly

100
Artist: **JACK PARDUE**
Art Director: Art Davis
Magazine: AOPA Pilot

98
Artist: **GUY BILLOUT**
Art Director: Colleen McCudden
Magazine: Insurance Review

99
Artist: **ANDRZEJ CZECZOT**
Art Director: Lee Lorenz
Magazine: The New Yorker

101
Artist: WILSON MCLEAN
Art Director: Judy Garlan
Magazine: Atlantic Monthly

102
Artist: **LANE SMITH**
Art Director: Joan Ferrell
Magazine: Travel and Leisure

103
Artist: **CHET RENESON**
Art Director: Gary Gretter
Magazine: Sports Afield

104 Artist: **JOHN THOMPSON** Art Director: Victor J. Closi Magazine: Field and Stream

105
Artist: **CHARLES REID**
Art Director: Gary Gretter
Magazine: Sports Afield

106
Artist: **GARY KELLEY**
Art Director: Fred Woodward
Magazine: Texas Monthly

107
Artist: **ROBERT HUNT**
Art Director: Ed Guthero
Magazine: Signs

108 Artist: **DAN ZAKROCZEMSKI** Art Director: John Davis Client: Buffalo News

109
Artist: **RICHARD SPARKS**
Art Director: Gary Gretter
Magazine: Sports Afield

110
Artist: **CAROL WALD**
Art Director: Julie Ris
Client: Michigan North Properties

111 Artist: **ELWYN MEHLMAN** Art Director: T.R. Fitchko Magazine: Capitol

112
Artist: **BECKY HEAVNER**
Art Director: Carla Frank
Magazine: Saturday Review

113 Artist: **FRANCES JETTER** Art Directors: Sara Whitford / Alan Richardson Magazine: Weight Watchers

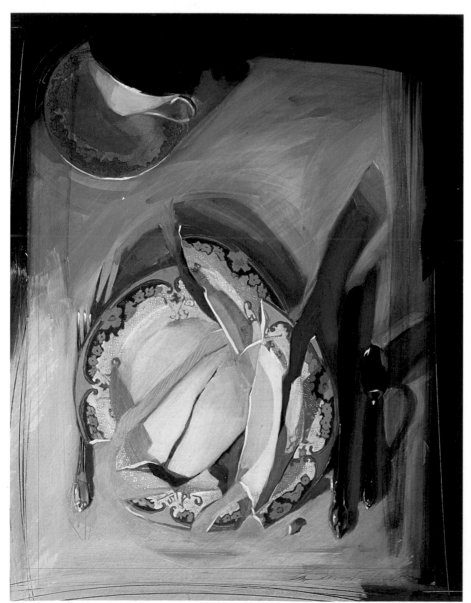

114
Artist: **SHELDON GREENBERG**
Art Director: Ken Kendrick
Magazine: The New York Times

115
Artist: **GWYN M. STRAMLER**
Art Director: Emily Borden
Magazine: Valley

116
Artist: **ANDREW SHACHAT**
Art Director: Lester Goodman
Magazine: Psychology Today

117
Artist: **PETER DE SÈVE**
Art Director: Lois Erlacher
Magazine: Emergency Medicine

119
Artist: **DAVID LEVINSON**

120
Artist: **DAVID SHANNON**
Art Director: Randy Jones
Client: United Features Syndicate

118
Artist: **DENISE WATT**
Art Director: Jim Groff
Magazine: Shell News

121 Artist: **CARY HENRIE**   Art Director: Mary Challinor   Magazine: Science '86

122
Artist: **MARK PENBERTHY**
Art Director: David Harris
Magazine: Dallas Times Herald

125 Artist: **JAMES ENDICOTT**   Art Director: Rosslyn Frick   Magazine: Byte

126
Artist: **JACK UNRUH**
Art Director: Jan Adkins
Magazine: National Geographic

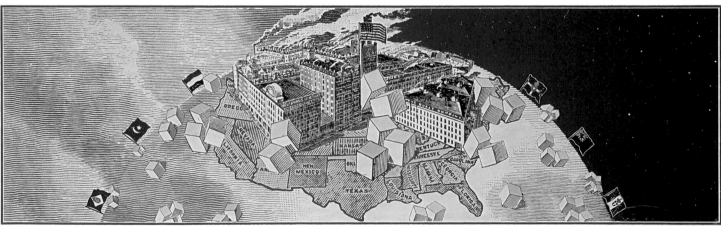

127
Artist: **JOHN CRAIG**
Art Director: Judy Garlan
Magazine: Atlantic Monthly

128
Artist: **KINUKO Y. CRAFT**
Art Director: Giona Miarella
Magazine: Adweek

129
Artist: **ANITA KUNZ**
Art Director: Ken Kendrick
Magazine: The New York Times

130
Artist: **BRAD HOLLAND**
Art Director: Robert Post
Magazine: Chicago

131 Artist: **GREG SPALENKA**   Art Director: Theo Kouvatsos   Magazine: Playboy

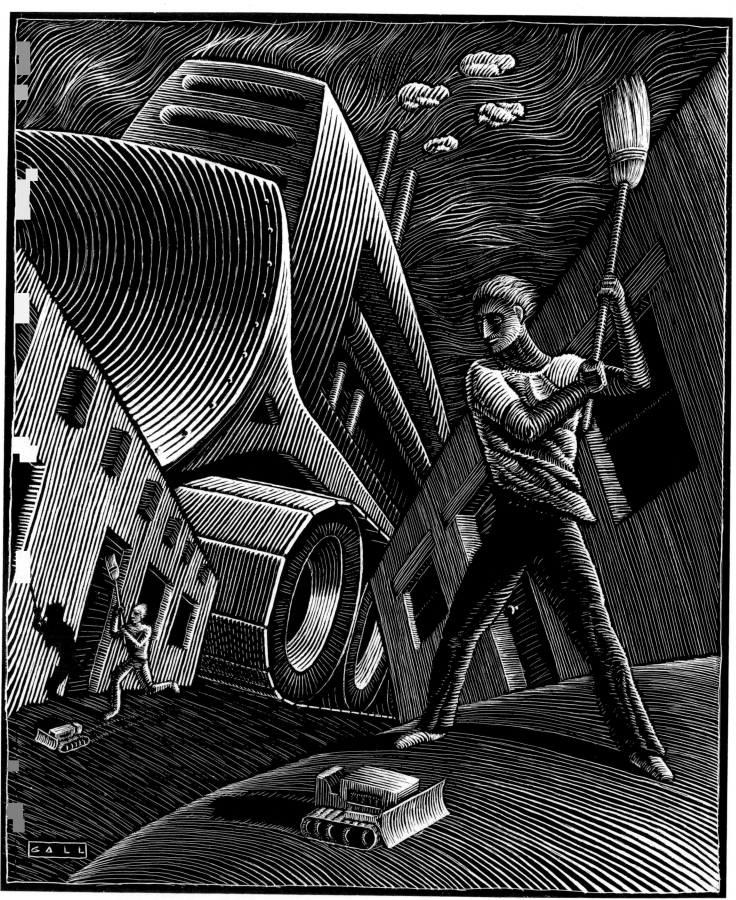

132 Artist: **CHRIS A. GALL**   Art Director: Chris A. Gall   Magazine: The Tucson Weekly

133
Artist: **GERRY GERSTEN**
Art Directors: Nick Meglin / Len Brenner
Magazine: Mad

134
Artist: **ALLEN HIRSCH**
Art Director: Rudy Hoglund
Magazine: Time

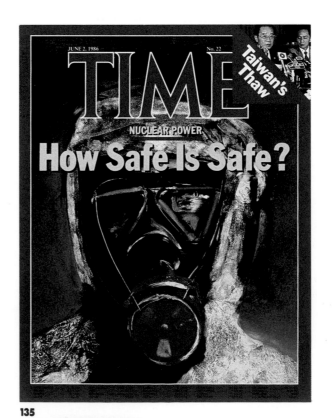

135
Artist: **MARSHALL ARISMAN**
Art Director: Rudy Hoglund
Magazine: Time

136
Artist: **STEVE BRODNER**
Art Director: Tom Staebler
Magazine: Playboy

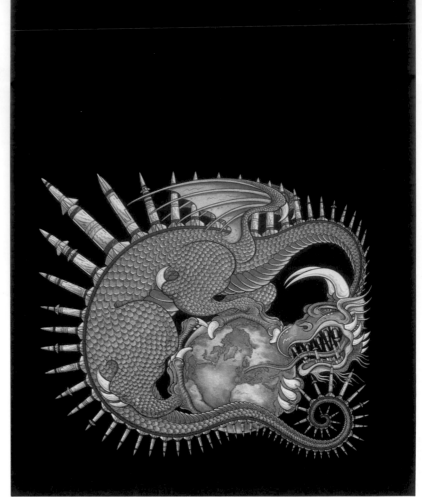

137
Artist: **JILL KARLA SCHWARZ**
Art Director: Nigel Holmes
Magazine: Time

138
Artist: **BOB SELBY**
Art Director: Mick Cochran
Magazine: Sunday Journal

139
Artist: **JEFF DODSON**
Art Director: April Silver
Magazine: Esquire

140
Artist: **BURT SILVERMAN**
Art Director: Rudy Hoglund
Magazine: Time

141 Artist: **JOHN CAMEJO**   Art Director: John Camejo   Magazine: Insight

142
Artist: **BURT SILVERMAN**
Art Director: Rudy Hoglund
Magazine: Time

SIR EDMOND HALLEY

143
Artist: **DANIEL MAFFIA**
Art Director: Shelley Heller
Magazine: Prestige Publications, Inc.

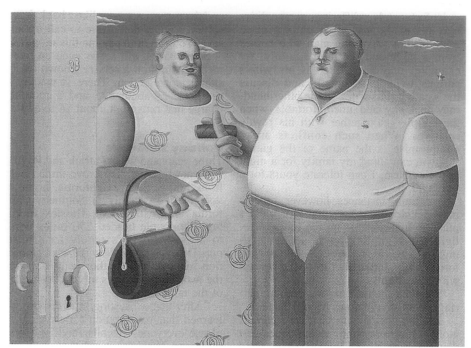

145
Artist: **SANDRA HENDLER**
Art Director: Evelyn Ellis
Magazine: New Marriage

146
Artist: **BRAD HOLLAND**
Art Director: Joan Hoffman
Magazine: Fortune

147
Artist: **PETER DE SÈVE**
Art Director: Roger Zapke
Magazine: Forbes

148
Artist: **PETER DE SÈVE**
Art Director: Lenore Cherney
Magazine: Inside

Roger Huyssen
Chairman
Illustrator

Sandy Kossin
Illustrator

Roberto Innocenti
Silver Medal

Richard Bleiweiss
Art Director,
Penthouse Magazine

Malcolm T. Liepke
Illustrator

Mel Odom
Silver Medal

Joe Connolly
Art Director, Boy's Life/
Boy Scouts of America

Marvin Mattelson
Illustrator

Richard Whitney
Silver Medal

Alex Ebel
Illustrator

Carmille Zaino
Illustrator

Kent Williams
Silver Medal

Joan Hall
Illustrator

Robert Wisnewski
Silver Medal

149 Artist: **ROBERTO INNOCENTI**   Art Director: Dale Pollekoff   Publisher: Time-Life Books

SILVER MEDAL

150   Artist: **MEL ODOM**   Art Director: Louise Fili   Publisher: Pantheon Books

SILVER MEDAL

151 Artist: **RICHARD WHITNEY**   Art Director: Richard Lack   Publisher: Taylor Publishing Co.

SILVER MEDAL

152　Artist: **KENT WILLIAMS**　Art Director: Neil Stuart　Publisher: Viking Penguin, Inc.

SILVER MEDAL

153 Artist: **ROBERT WISNEWSKI**
SILVER MEDAL

154
Artist: **JEANNE FISHER**
Art Directors: Judith Loeser / Carin Goldberg
Publisher: Vintage Books

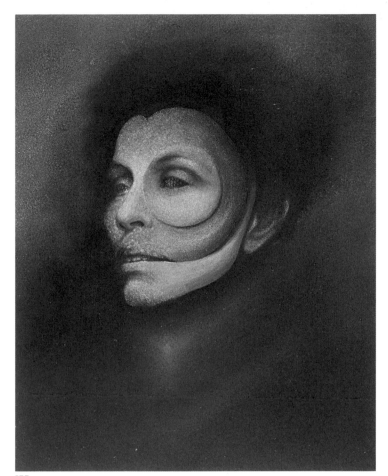

155
Artist: **RALPH MASIELLO**
Art Director: Neil Stuart
Publisher: Viking Penguin, Inc.

156
Artist: **RON LESSER**
Art Director: Bruce Hall
Publisher: Pocket Books

157
Artist: **RICK KRONINGER**

158
Artist: **KENT WILLIAMS**
Art Director: Neil Stuart
Publisher: Viking Penguin, Inc.

159
Artist: **MARK LEFKOWITZ**

160 Artist: **MICHAEL DEAS** Art Director: David Tommasino Publisher: Scholastic, Inc.

161
Artist: **STAN HUNTER**

162 Artist: **RICK LOVELL**   Art Director: Judith Loeser   Publisher: Vintage Books

163 Artist: **JOHN JINKS**   Art Director: Krystyna Skalski   Publisher: Bantam Books

164 Artist: **SHERILYN VANVALKENBURGH** Art Director: Michael Mendelsohn Publisher: Franklin Library

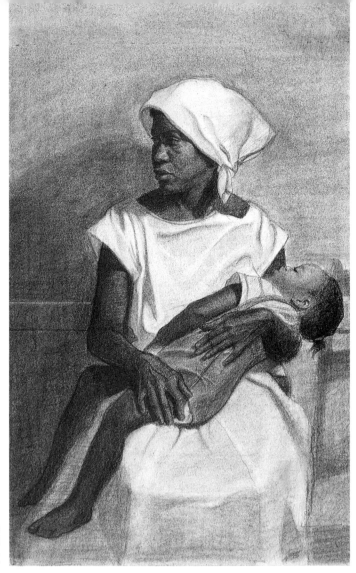

165
Artist: **ERIC VELASQUEZ**
Art Director: Terry Moogan
Publisher: Harper and Row

166 Artist: **KIMANNE UHLER**

167 Artist: **KAREN BARBOUR**   Art Director: Vaughn Andrews   Publisher: Harcourt Brace Jovanovich

168   Artist: **JIM SPANFELLER**   Art Directors: Michael Mendelsohn / Jennifer Dossin   Publisher: Franklin Library

169 Artist: **ANITA KUNZ**   Art Director: Gerald Counihan   Publisher: Dell Publishing Co., Inc.

170 Artist: **PHIL HULING**   Art Director: Frank Metz   Publisher: Simon & Schuster

171
Artist: **ELAINE RAPHAEL/DON BOLOGNESE**
Art Director: Michael Mendelsohn
Publisher: Franklin Library

172
Artist: **PHIL HULING**
Art Director: Frank Metz
Publisher: Simon & Schuster

174
Artist: **ED ACUNA**
Art Director: Richard Carter
Publisher: Easton Press

175
Artist: **C.F. PAYNE**
Art Director: Fred Woodward
Publisher: Texas Monthly

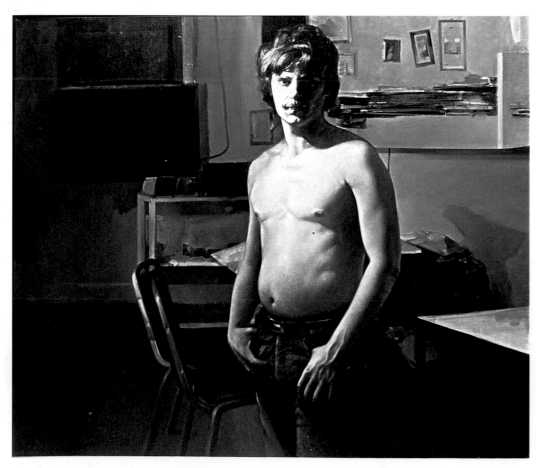

176
Artist: **MOHAMED DRISI**

178 Artist: **RICHARD JESSE WATSON**   Art Director: Joy Chu   Publisher: Harcourt Brace Jovanovich

179
Artist: **MAX GINSBURG**
Art Director: Marva Martin
Publisher: Bantam Books

180
Artist: **LINDA BENSON**
Art Director: Atha Tehon
Publisher: Dial Books for Young Readers

182 Artist: **ROBERT SCHULMAN**

183
Artist: **JERRY PINKNEY**
Art Director: Soren Noring
Publisher: Reader's Digest

184 Artist: **RICHARD WILLIAMS**   Art Director: David Tommasino   Publisher: Scholastic, Inc.

185   Artist: **RICHARD JESSE WATSON**   Art Director: Joy Chu   Publisher: Harcourt Brace Jovanovich

187 Artist: **ROBERTO INNOCENTI**   Art Director: Dale Pollekoff   Publisher: Time-Life Books

188
Artist: **DENNIS LUZAK**
Art Director: Barbara Buck

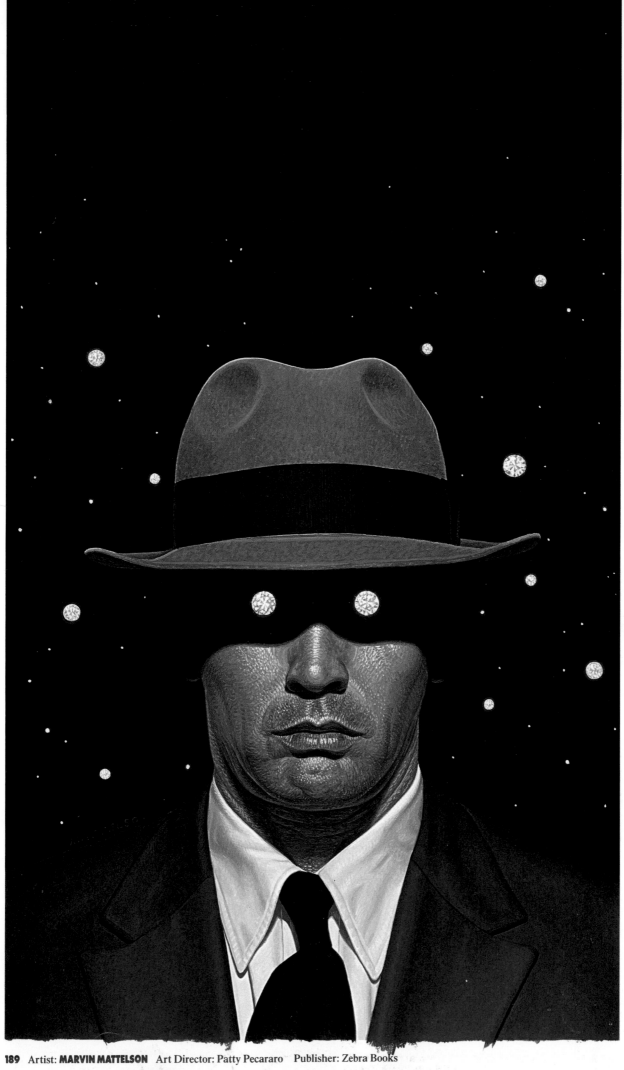

189 Artist: **MARVIN MATTELSON** Art Director: Patty Pecararo Publisher: Zebra Books

191
Artist: **JOHN SPOSATO**
Art Director: Robert Aulicino
Publisher: Random House

192
Artist: **MITCHELL HOOKS**
Art Director: Ruth Ross
Publisher: Ballantine Books

190
Artist: **ROBERT CRAWFORD**
Art Director: Neil Stuart
Publisher: Viking Penguin, Inc.

193
Artist: **MITCHELL HOOKS**
Art Director: Ruth Ross
Publisher: Ballantine Books

194
Artist: **GREG SPALENKA**
Art Director: Dorothy Schmidt
Publisher: Reader's Digest

196
Artist: **GREG SPALENKA**
Art Director: Dorothy Schmidt
Publisher: Reader's Digest

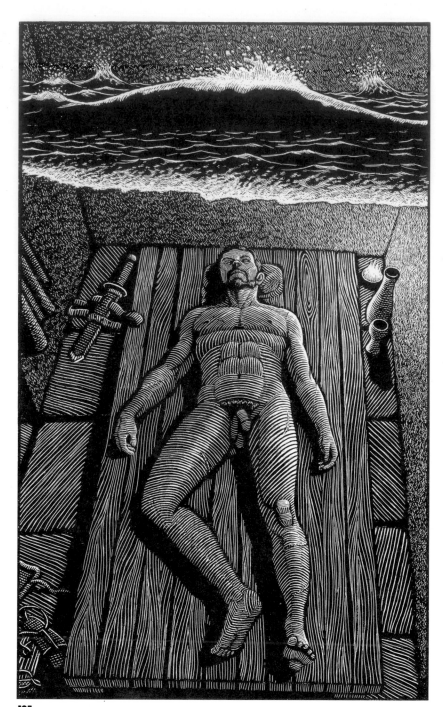

195
Artist: **DOUGLAS SMITH**
Publisher: Arkham House Publishers, Inc.

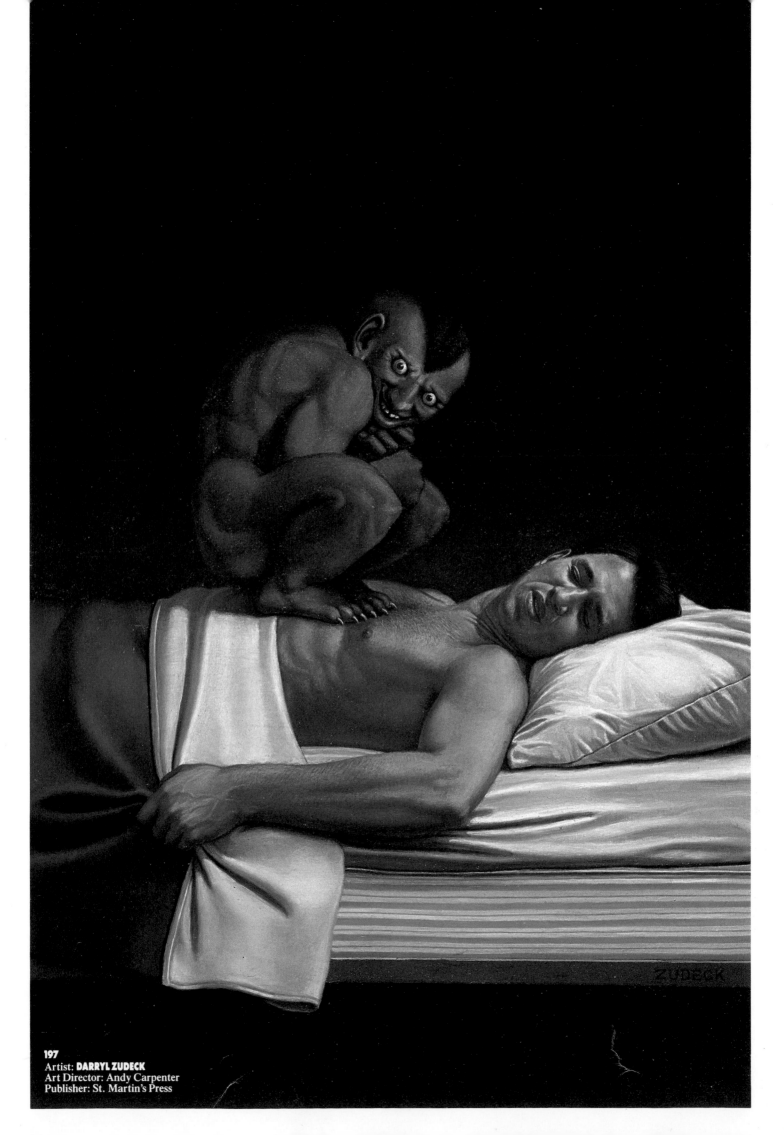

197
Artist: **DARRYL ZUDECK**
Art Director: Andy Carpenter
Publisher: St. Martin's Press

198
Artist: **CHRISTOPHER ZACHAROW**
Art Director: Joseph Montebello
Publisher: Harper and Row

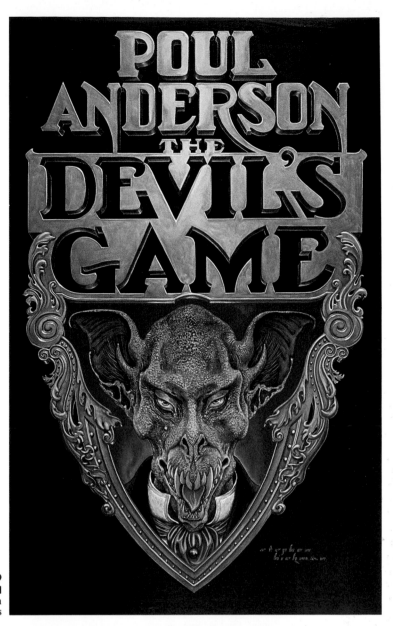

199
Artist: **STEPHEN HICKMAN**
Art Director: Jim Baen
Publisher: Baen Books

200
Artist: **LARS HOKANSON / LOIS HOKANSON**
Art Director: Sara Eisenman
Publisher: Alfred A. Knopf

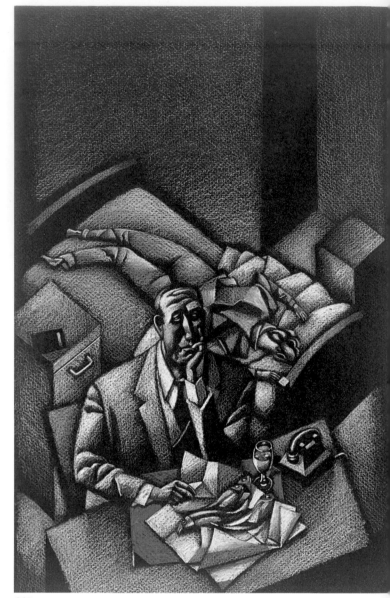

201
Artist: **JOHN HOWARD**
Art Director: Krystyna Skalski
Publisher: Bantam Books

202
Artist: **JOHN HOWARD**
Art Director: Milton Charles
Publisher: Pocket Books

203 Artist: **RICHARD BOBER**   Art Director: George Cornell   Client: New American Library

204 Artist: **TERESA FASOLINO** Art Director: Robert Aulicino Publisher: Random House

205
Artist: **MAX GINSBURG**
Art Directors: Bruce Hall / Patty Eslinger
Publisher: Pocket Books

206   Artist: **RUTH SANDERSON**   Art Directors: Armand Eisen / Tom Durwood   Publisher: Alfred A. Knopf/Ariel Books

EXIT TO EDEN
A NOVEL

207 Artist: **MEL ODOM** Art Director: Dorothy Wachtenheim Publisher: Arbor House

209
Artist: **MAX GINSBURG**
Art Director: Jackie Meyers
Publisher: Warner Books

208
Artist: **RICHARD WHITNEY**
Art Director: Richard Lack
Publisher: Taylor Publishing Co.

210 Artist: **THOMAS CANTY** Art Director: George Cornell Publisher: New American Library

211　Artist: **MEL ODOM**　Art Director: Victor Weaver　Publisher: Dell Publishing Co., Inc.

212 Artist: **MEL ODOM**   Art Director: George Cornell   Publisher: New American Library

213 Artist: **RUTH SANDERSON**   Art Directors: Armand Eisen / Tom Durwood   Publisher: Alfred A. Knopf/Ariel Books

214
Artist: **GLENN BATKIN**

215
Artist: **ALLEN GARNS**

216
Artist: **TOM HALLMAN**
Art Director: Jim Plumeri
Publisher: Bantam Books

217 Artist: **RUTH SANDERSON**   Art Directors: Armand Eisen / Tom Durwood   Publisher: Alfred A. Knopf / Ariel Books

218 Artist: **ROBERT A. OLSON** Art Director: Robert A. Olson Client: Windemere Galleries

219
Artist: **RICK MUJICA**

221 Artist: **JIMMY HARRIS**

222 Artist: **CHARLES SANTORE** Art Director: Elizabeth Zozom Publisher: Running Press

Artist: **DAN REED**
Art Director: Joseph Montebello
Publisher: Harper and Row

223 Artist: **ED LINDLOF**   Art Director: Neil Stuart   Publisher: Viking Penguin, Inc.

224 Artist: **JÖZEF SUMICHRAST** Art Director: Carol Mendelson

225 Artist: **CHARLES SANTORE** Art Director: Elizabeth Zozom Publisher: Running Press

226 Artist: **JANE PINKNEY** Art Director: Riki Levinson Publisher: E.P. Dutton Children's Books

227
Artist: **JOHN SANDFORD**
Art Director: Richard Pape
Publisher: Schoolzone Publishing

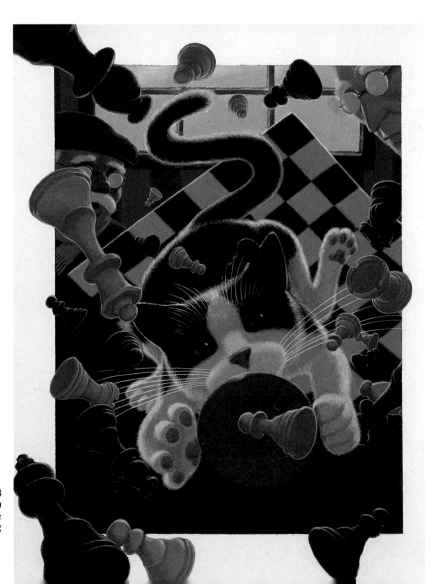

228
Artist: **JOHN SANDFORD**
Art Director: Richard Pape
Publisher: Schoolzone Publishing

229
Artist: **VINCE NATALE**

230 Artist: **BRALDT BRALDS**   Art Director: Betsy Wollheim   Publisher: Daw Books

231 Artist: **ROBERT GOLDSTROM**   Art Director: Krystyna Skalski   Publisher: Bantam Books

232
Artist: **JOHN RUSH**
Art Director: Gerry Counihan
Publisher: Dell Publishing Co., Inc.

233 Artist: **GARY KELLEY**   Art Director: Mary Staples   Publisher: Time-Life Books

234 Artist: **JERRY LOFARO**   Art Director: Neil Stuart   Publisher: Viking Penguin, Inc.

235 Artist: **DAVID TAMURA**   Art Director: Joseph Montebello   Publisher: Harper and Row

236
Artist: **NICHOLAS WILTON**
Art Director: Neil Stuart
Publisher: Viking Penguin, Inc.

237
Artist: **JOHN D. DAWSON**
Art Director: Christine Brundage
Client: Ortho Books

239 Artist: **JOHN JINKS**   Art Director: Krystyna Skalski   Publisher: Bantam Books

240 Artist: **CHRISTOPHER ZACHAROW**   Art Director: Neil Stuart   Publisher: Viking Penguin, Inc.

241 Artist: **COLLETTE SLADE**   Art Director: Gene Mydlowski   Publisher: Berkley Publishing Group

242 Artist: **DOUGLAS FRASER** Art Director: Sara Eisenman Publisher: Alfred A. Knopf

243 Artist: **MALCOLM T. LIEPKE**

244
Artist: **ED LINDLOF**
Art Director: Melissa Jacoby
Publisher: Viking Penguin, Inc.

245 Artist: **VICTOR ANONSEN**

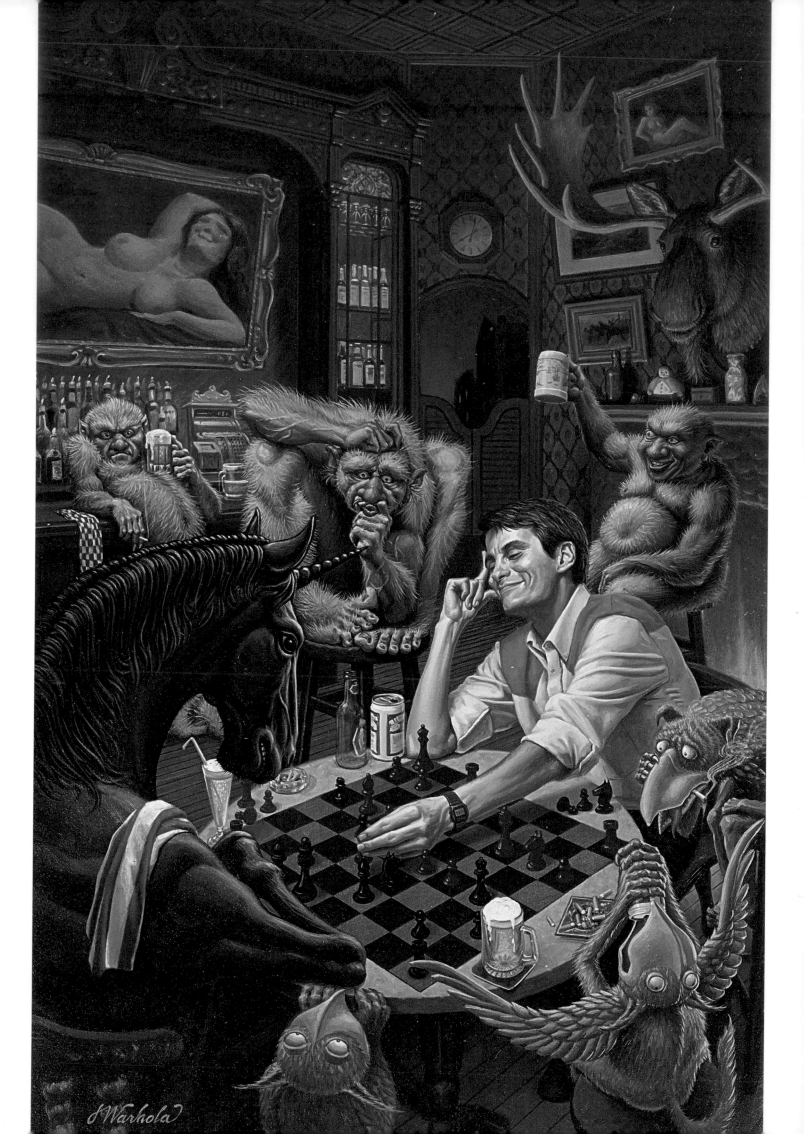

247
Artist: **WENDELL MINOR**
Art Director: Vaughn Andrews
Publisher: Harcourt Brace Jovanovich

246
Artist: **JAMES WARHOLA**
Art Director: Matt Tepper
Publisher: Avon Books

248
Artist: **JOHN MAZZINI**
Art Director: Pearl Lau
Publisher: Little, Brown & Co.

Pietzsch 85

250
Artist: **WENDELL MINOR**
Art Director: Jackie Meyer
Publisher: MacMillan Publishing Co.

251
Artist: **ETIENNE DELESSERT**
Art Director: Rita Marshall
Client: Gael Towey

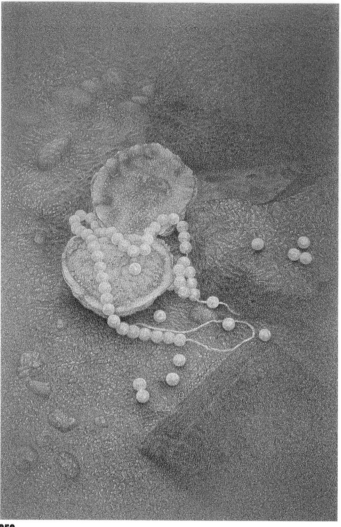

252
Artist: **LINDA BENSON**
Art Director: Neil Stuart
Publisher: Viking Penguin, Inc.

253
Artist: **ROBERT CRAWFORD**
Art Director: Neil Stuart
Publisher: Viking Penguin, Inc.

254
Artist: **MARY S. FLOCK**

255
Artist: **TIMOTHY JONKE**
Art Director: David Mocarski
Client: Art Center College of Design

257 Artist: **WILLIAM GEORGE**

256
Artist: **CHRISTOPHER ZACHOROW**
Art Director: Neil Stuart
Publisher: Viking Penguin, Inc.

258
Artist: **BART FORBES**
Art Director: Angelo Perrone
Publisher: Reader's Digest

259 Artist: **ED LINDLOF**   Art Director: Frederick Barthelme   Client: University of Southern Mississippi

260
Artist: **ETIENNE DELESSERT**
Art Director: Rita Marshall
Client: Stewart, Tabori & Chang

261 Artist: **JEFFREY WALKER** Art Director: Asher Kingsley Publisher: Ballantine Books

262
Artist: **WENDELL MINOR**
Art Director: Ruth Kolbert
Publisher: Scribner's

263
Artist: **STEPHEN A. WAGNER**

264 Artist: **ROBERT CRAWFORD** Art Director: Joseph Montebello Publisher: Harper and Row

265
Artist: **WILLIAM LOW**
Art Director: Neil Stuart
Publisher: Viking Penguin, Inc.

266 Artist: **RICHARD WHITNEY** Art Director: Richard Lack Publisher: Taylor Publishing Co.

267 Artist: **JEFFREY WALKER** Art Director: Asher Kingsley Publisher: Ballantine Books

268 Artist: **AJIN** Art Director: Sara Eisenman Publisher: Alfred A. Knopf

269
Artist: **DAVID SHANNON**
Art Director: Darcie Furlan
Publisher: Microsoft Press

270
Artist: **MICHAEL SCHUMACHER**
Art Director: Neil Stuart
Client: Viking Penguin, Inc.

271 Artist: **WILLIAM HANSON**

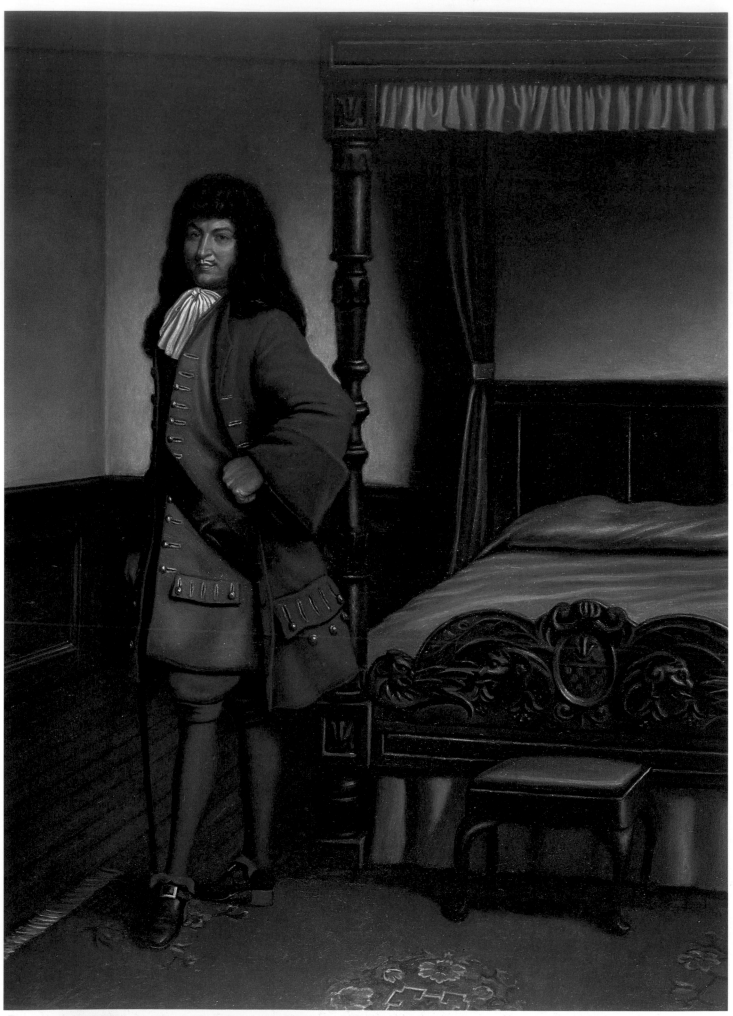

272 Artist: **DARRYL ZUDECK** Art Directors: Paolo Pepe / Andy Carpenter Publisher: St. Martin's Press

273 Artist: **JIM HEATER**

274
Artist: **DAVID FRAMPTON**
Art Director: Dorothy Schmidt
Publisher: Reader's Digest General Books

275
Artist: **BOB SABIN**
Art Director: Don Munson
Publisher: Ballantine Books

276 Artist: **RICK LOVELL**   Art Director: Judith Loeser   Publisher: Vintage Books

277
Artist: **FRED MARCELLINO**
Art Director: Louise Fili
Publisher: Pantheon Books

278
Artist: **TOM SCIACCA**
Art Director: Krystyna Skalski
Publisher: Bantam Books

279 Artist: **STEPHEN HICKMAN**   Art Director: Jim Baen   Publisher: Baen Books

280
Artist: **NORBERT IVANYI**
Art Director: Matt Tepper
Publisher: Avon Books

281   Artist: **ROBERT LO GRIPPO**

282 Artist: **RALPH MASIELLO**   Art Director: Neil Stuart   Publisher: Viking Penguin, Inc.

283
Artist: **WILSON McLEAN**
Art Director: Jack Odette
Client: Citicorp

284
Artist: **FLOYD COOPER**
Publisher: Harcourt Brace Jovanovich

285
Artist: **KAM MAK**
Art Director: Lee Wade
Publisher: Macmillan Publishing Co.

286 Artist: **CHRIS HOPKINS**   Art Director: Jamie Warren   Publisher: Bantam Books

287 Artist: **JERRY LOFARO**   Art Director: Jamie Warren   Publisher: Bantam Books

288　Artist: **JERRY LOFARO**　Art Director: Neil Stuart　Publisher: Viking Penguin, Inc.

290
Artist: **RICHARD BERRY**
Art Director: Gene Mydlowski
Publisher: Berkley Publishing Group

291
Artist: **TIM HILDEBRANDT**
Art Director: George Cornell
Publisher: Signet Books

292
Artist: **ROBERT HUNT**
Art Director: George Cornell
Publisher: New American Library

289
Artist: **RALPH McQUARRIE**
Art Directors: Alex Jay / Byron Preiss
Publisher: Berkley Publishing Group

293
Artist: **JOHN JUDE PALENCAR**
Art Directors: Dale Pollekoff / Louis Klein
Publisher: Time-Life Books

294
Artist: **DOUGLAS SMITH**
Publisher: Arkham House Publishers, Inc.

295
Artist: **JOHN JUDE PALENCAR**
Art Directors: Dale Pollekoff / Louis Klein
Publisher: Time-Life Books

296
Artist: **TOM SCIACCA**
Art Director: Krystyna Skalski
Publisher: Bantam Books

297
Artist: **PAUL ZELINSKY**
Art Director: Riki Levinson
Publisher: E.P. Dutton Children's Books

298 Artist: **ROBERT McGINNIS** Art Director: Marion Davis Publisher: Reader's Digest

Alvin Pimsler
Chairman
Illustrator

Richard Sparks
Illustrator

Victor Closi
Art Director, Field & Stream

Simms Taback
Illustrator

Keith Ferris
Illustrator

J. Robert Teringo
Art Director, National
Geographic Magazine

Rudolph Hoglund
Art Director, Time Magazine

Dorothy
Wachtenheim
Art Director,
Arbor House Publishing Co.

Dennis Lyall
Illustrator

Bradlt Bralds
Gold Medal

Brad Holland
Silver Medal

Kinuko Craft
Gold Medal

Kunio Hagio
Gold Medal

Joe Saffold
Gold Medal

Robert M.
Cunningham
Silver Medal

29 ADVERTISING

299 Artist: **BRALDT BRALDS**   Art Directors: Nancy Rice / Ricardo Van Steen   Agency: Rice and Rice Advertising / CVS Comunicaciones   Client: Minneapolis Art Directors Club

300 Artist: **KINUKO Y. CRAFT**   Art Directors: Randy Papke / Ken Sakoda   Agency: Salvati Montgomery Sakoda, Inc.   Client: ITT

GOLD MEDAL / HAMILTON KING AWARD

301 Artist: **KUNIO HAGIO**   Art Director: Marty Gustavson   Agency: Leo Burnett   Client: United Airlines

GOLD MEDAL

302 Artist: **JOE SAFFOLD** Art Director: Steve Martin Agency: Young and Martin Client: Charter Hospital of Long Beach

GOLD MEDAL

303 Artist: **ROBERT M. CUNNINGHAM** Art Director: Pat Farrell Agency: Austin Kelley Advertising Client: Dataw Island/ALCOA

SILVER MEDAL

304 Artist: **BRAD HOLLAND** Art Director: Bill Freeland Client: City University of New York

SILVER MEDAL

305
Artist: **RICHARD MANTEL**
Art Director: Siran Kaprielian
Agency: Kaprielian O'Leary
Client: F.A. Spina & Company, Inc.

306
Artist: **DON WELLER**
Art Directors: Don Weller / Harold Burch
Client: Sinclair Printing

307 Artist: **BILL MAYER** Art Director: Rick Anywil Agency: Creative Services Client: Graphic Ads

Artist: **DALE C. VERZAAL**
Client: Butler Paper Co.

on a lark

309
Artist: **CONNIE CONNALLY**
Art Director: Jon Gregory
Client: Fontana Center

310
Artist: **JEFFREY TERRESON**
Art Director: Bob Dunnigan
Client: Enco Printing Products

312
Artist: **ALAN PHILLIPS**

313
Artist: **MARTIN BRUINSMA**
Art Director: Barry E. Jackson
Client: Warner Brothers Records

311
Artist: **BRALDT BRALDS**
Art Directors: Victor Vorderstrasse / Tom Birkenmeier
Agency: B.F.V. & L. Advertising
Client: Bols Liquers

314 Artist: **KAREN FARYNIAK**   Art Director: Donna Albert   Agency: Ketchum Advertising   Client: Pennsylvania Tours

315 Artist: **BILL MAYER**   Art Director: Dave Curtis   Agency: Richardson Myers Donofrio   Client: Haver

316 Artist: **STEVE BRODNER**   Art Director: Joseph Stelmach   Client: RCA Records

317
Artist: **JEFF SEAVER**
Art Director: Bernie Hogya
Agency: Bozelle & Jacobs
Client: Alpine

318
Artist: **CHARLES SANTORE**
Art Director: Elizabeth Zozom
Client: Courage Books

319 Artist: **EDWARD GAZSI** Art Director: George Courides, Jr. Agency: Thomas G. Ferguson Associates Client: Warner Lambert/EPT Plus

320 Artist: **EDWARD GAZSI** Art Director: George Courides, Jr. Agency: Thomas G. Ferguson Associates Client: Warner Lambert/EPT Plus

321
Artist: **JEFFREY TERRESON**
Art Director: Bob Dunnigan
Client: Enco Printing Products

322 Artist: **EZRA N. TUCKER** Art Director: Steve Stone Agency: Ketchum Advertising Client: Great America

323 Artist: **TED LEWIN**   Art Director: Stephanie Naas Lyons   Agency: FCB-LKP Advertising   Client: Lenox Collections

324 Artist: **ROBERT GIUSTI**   Art Director: Mark Barensfeld   Agency: Schenker, Probst, Barensfeld   Client: Cincinnati Zoo

325 Artist: **ROBERT GANTT STEELE**   Art Directors: John Carter / Dorothy Allard   Agency: Evans Weinberg, Inc.   Client: Beverly Hills Hotel

326
Artist: **CHARLES WATERHOUSE**
Art Director: Bob Brennan
Client: Sackett's Harbor Historical Foundation

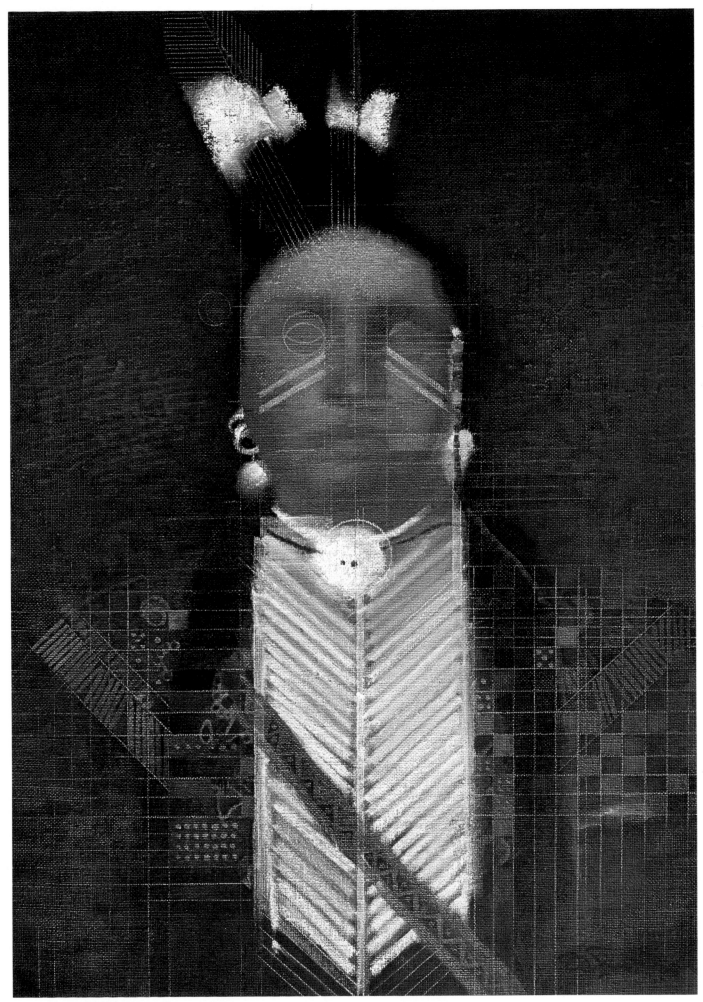

327 Artist: **MARK ENGLISH**   Art Director: Bob Paige   Agency: Paige Group   Client: Mohawk Paper

328 Artist: **JAMES McMULLAN**   Art Director: Ken Garrison   Client: Simpson Paper

329
Artist: **M. JOHN ENGLISH**
Art Director: Mark English
Client: Prince of Prints

330
Artist: **M. JOHN ENGLISH**
Art Director: Mark English
Client: Prince of Prints

331 Artist: **KAZUHIKO SANO**   Art Director: Robert Hendricks   Agency: Carter / Callahan   Client: Grovesnor Development

332 Artist: **GEORGE S. GAADT**   Art Director: Keith Andrus   Client: Sullivan Gray and Riat, Inc.

333 Artist: **DOUGLAS FRASER** Art Director: Evan Peter Agency: Vilas Advertising, Inc. Client: Tasco Industries

334 Artist: **MICHAEL SWAINE** Art Director: Ann Hubbard Agency: Hubbard & Hubbard
Client: The Arizona Portfolio

335 Artist: **MARK ENGLISH**   Art Director: Clare Frances   Agency: Needham Porter Novelli

336
Artist: **DON SIBLEY**
Art Director: Don Sibley
Client: Herring Marathon Group

337
Artist: **DON SIBLEY**
Art Director: Don Sibley
Client: Herring Marathon Group

338
Artist: **DON SIBLEY**
Art Director: Don Sibley
Client: Good Advertising / Federal Express

339 Artist: **DOUG JOHNSON**   Art Directors: Judy Kurbidge / Doug Johnson   Client: Smithsonian Institute / Sites

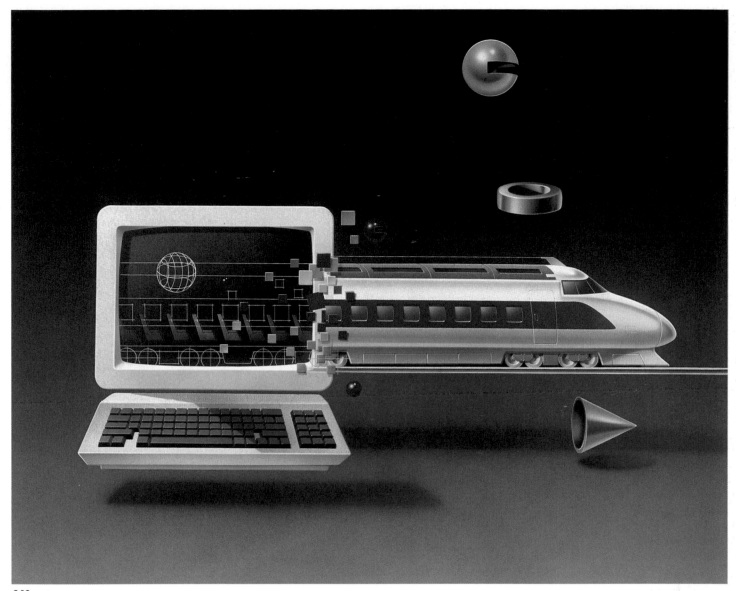

340
Artist: **THEO RUDNAK**
Art Director: Gary Lancaster
Client: Engineer Works

341
Artist: **KEVIN BURKE**
Art Director: Tim Smith
Client: B.F. Goodrich

342
Artist: **DON KUEKER**
Art Director: Art Maas
Agency: Busch Creative Services
Client: Anheuser-Busch

343 Artist: **BERNIE FUCHS** Art Director: Andy Molnar Client: Cadillac

344
Artist: **ROBERT M. CUNNINGHAM**
Art Director: Ron Sullivan
Client: Trammell Crow Company

345
Artist: **FRANCIS LIVINGSTON**
Art Director: Kim Carter
Agency: Dalin Smith White
Client: Novell

346
Artist: **EZRA N. TUCKER**
Art Director: David C. Bartels
Agency: Bartels and Carstens
Client: Anheuser-Busch

347
Artist: **WENDELL MINOR**
Art Director: Matt Tepper
Client: Avon Books

348
Artist: **FRANCIS LIVINGSTON**
Art Director: Christy Neal
Client: Four Seasons Hotel

349
Artist: **RICK McCOLLUM**
Art Director: Jack Lanza
Agency: The Morgan Agency
Client: Travenol/Healthcare Information Services

350
Artist: **STEVE JOHNSON**
Art Director: Thom Sandberg
Agency: The Kenyon Consortium
Client: University of Minnesota Film Society

351 Artist: **MICHAEL GARLAND**

352
Artist: **WILSON McLEAN**
Art Director: Koji Tanaka
Client: Budweiser Beer

353
Artist: **JEAN PROBERT**
Art Director: Jim White
Agency: D'Arcy Masius Benton and Bowles
Client: Anheuser-Busch

354
Artist: **WILSON McLEAN**
Art Director: Koji Tanaka
Client: Budweiser Beer

355 Artist: **ROBERT M. CUNNINGHAM** Art Director: Pat Farrell Agency: Austin Kelley Advertising Client: Dataw Island / ALCOA

356
Artist: **DON KUEKER**
Art Director: Art Maas
Agency: Busch Creative Services
Client: Anheuser-Busch

357
Artist: **EZRA N. TUCKER**
Art Director: Laury Wolfe
Agency: McCann Erickson
Client: Coca-Cola Classic

358
Artist: **ROBERT HEINDEL**
Art Director: George Pierson
Client: Home Box Office

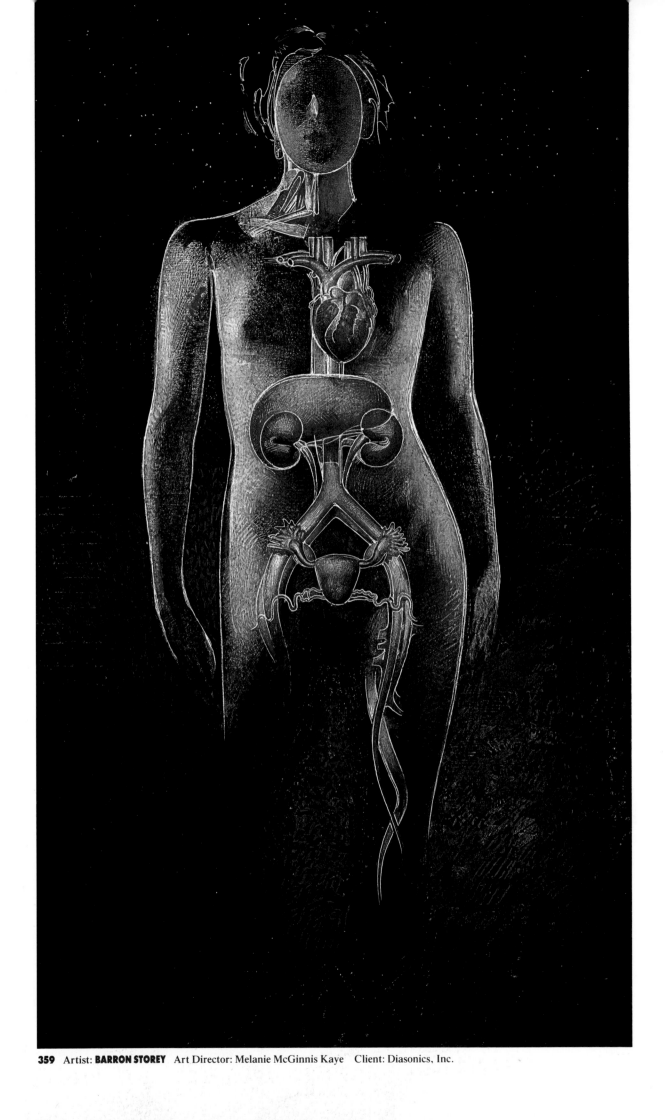

359 Artist: **BARRON STOREY**   Art Director: Melanie McGinnis Kaye   Client: Diasonics, Inc.

360 Artist: **MELISSA GRIMES**   Art Director: Richard Whittington   Agency: Whittington, Meis & Narro

361
Artist: **DAN H. BRAWNER**
Art Director: Kent Hunter
Client: Reunion Records

362 Artist: **MARK A. FREDRICKSON**   Art Director: Anne Hubbard   Agency: Hubbard & Hubbard   Client: Arizona Portfolio

364
Artist: **MARK HESS / RICHARD HESS**
Art Director: Bob Barrie
Agency: Fallon Mc Elligot Rice
Client: Prince Spaghetti

363
Artist: **MARCO J. VENTURA**
Art Director: Piero Ventura
Client: Antiche Fattorie Fiorentine

365 Artist: **ANTONIO WADE** Art Director: Mark Lang Client: Maritz Motivation Co.

366 Artist: **FRED OTNES** Art Director: Bob Defrin Client: Atlantic Records

367 Artist: **FRED OTNES** Art Director: Bob Defrin Client: Atlantic Records

368
Artist: **APRIL GOODMAN-WILLY**
Art Director: April Goodman-Willy
Client: Clowes Memorial Hall

369
Artist: **KAREN FARYNIAK**
Art Director: Donna Albert
Agency: Ketchum Advertising
Client: Pennsylvania Tours

370 Artist: **ROBERT HEINDEL** Art Director: Philip Arnott Client: The Stable Gallery

371 Artist: **MARK ENGLISH** Art Director: Roger Coleman Client: Westport Allen Center

372 Artist: **ROBERT HEINDEL** Art Director: Philip Arnott Client: The Stable Gallery

373
Artist: **ALLEN GARNS**
Art Director: Kent Looft
Agency: L & M Advertising
Client: Phoenix Symphony

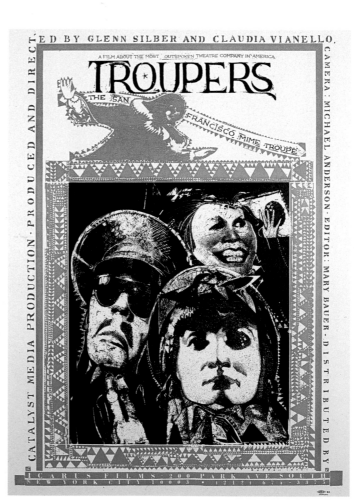

374
Artist: **BARRON STOREY**
Art Director: Barron Storey
Client: Glenn Silber

375
Artist: **ROBERT A. OLSON**
Art Director: Robert A. Olson
Client: Windemere Galleries

376
Artist: **ROBERT HEINDEL**
Art Director: Philip Arnott
Client: The Stable Gallery

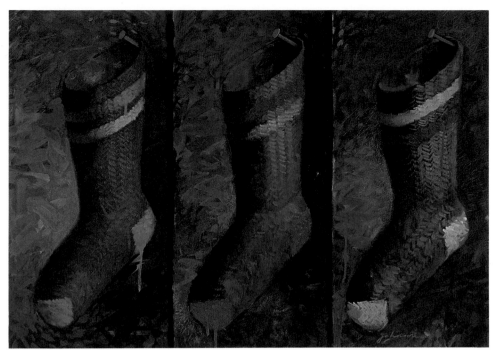

377
Artist: **STEVE JOHNSON**
Art Director: George Halvorson
Agency: Key Group Advertising
Client: Norwest Center

378
Artist: **JACQUELINE JASPER**
Art Director: Ann Marie Light
Agency: Ephron, Raboy, Tsao
Client: Alcott and Andrews

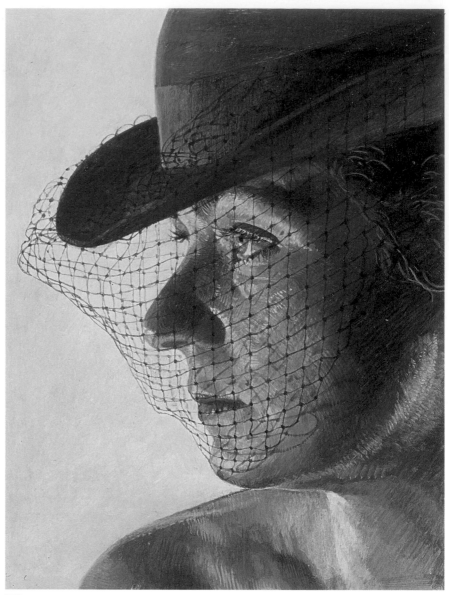

379
Artist: **JOHN THOMPSON**

380   Artist: **KUNIO HAGIO**   Art Director: Marty Gustavson   Agency: Leo Burnett   Client: United Airlines

Artist: **GARY KELLE**
Art Director: Gary Kelle
Client: Western Michigan University Theatr

382 Artist: **ROB DAY**   Art Directors: David Young / Jeff Laramore   Agency: Young and Laramore   Client: J.C. Sipe Jewelers

383
Artist: **MICHAEL CONWAY**

384
Artist: **LESLIE WU**
Art Director: Bruce Kielar
Agency: Perri Debes Looney & Crane Advertising, Inc.
Client: Finger Lakes Wine Cellars, Inc.

385
Artist: **BRAD HOLLAND**
Art Director: Brad Holland
Client: Tulsa Art Directors Club

386
Artist: **MARK LANGENECKERT**
Art Director: Jack Thorwegan
Agency: The Zipatoni Co.
Client: First Annual St. Louis Advertising Exposition

387
Artist: **EDWARD ABRAMS**
Art Director: Marvin Schwartz
Client: Angel Records

388
Artist: **BURT SILVERMAN**
Art Director: Peggy Pettus
Agency: McCaffrey & McCall, Inc.
Client: PBS/Exxon

389
Artist: **PAUL DAVIS**
Art Director: Paul Davis
Client: The New York Shakespeare Festival

390
Artist: **MARVIN MATTELSON**
Art Director: David Hunter
Agency: Foote, Cone & Belding
Client: Pacific Telesis

391
Artist: **RONALD N. SHERR**

392
Artist: **JON FLAMING**
Art Director: Ron Sullivan
Agency: Sullivan Perkins
Client: The Rouse Company

393 Artist: **DAVID BEYNON PENA** Art Director: Gail Zambor Agency: Louis Scott Associates Client: Chemical Bank

395
Artist: **JOE SAFFOLD**
Art Director: Steve Martin
Agency: Young and Martin
Client: Charter Hospital of Long Beach

394
Artist: **JOE SAFFOLD**
Art Director: Steve Martin
Agency: Young and Martin
Client: Charter Hospital of Long Beach

396
Artist: **C. ROYD CROSTHWAITE**
Art Director: C. Royd Crosthwaite
Client: Frank and Jeff Lavaty

397 Artist: **JOEL SPECTOR** Art Director: Steve Rousso Agency: Rousso and Wagner Client: Elkay Real Estate Properties

398
Artist: **JOHN THOMPSON**
Art Director: Tom Demeter
Agency: Cosmopulos, Crowley and Daly, Inc.
Client: Allendale Insurance

399
Artist: **WAYNE WATFORD**
Art Directors: Roger Corman / Julie Corman
Client: Concorde/Cinema Group

400
Artist: **DENIS PARKHURST**
Art Director: Ken Parkhurst
Client: Scott and Scott Lithography

401   Artist: **VICTOR JUHASZ**   Art Director: Pat Epstein   Agency: Scali Mc Cabe Sloves, Inc.   Client: Continental Airlines

402
Artist: **JEFF DODSON**
Art Director: Jodi Donato
Client: CBS Masterworks

403 Artist: **ROB DAY** Art Directors: David Young / Jeff Laramore   Client: Young and Laramore

404 Artist: **ROB DAY** Art Directors: David Young / Jeff Laramore Client: Young and Laramore

405
Artist: **LOU MYERS**
Art Director: Joe Loconto
Agency: Dancer Fitzgerald
Client: Yellow Pages

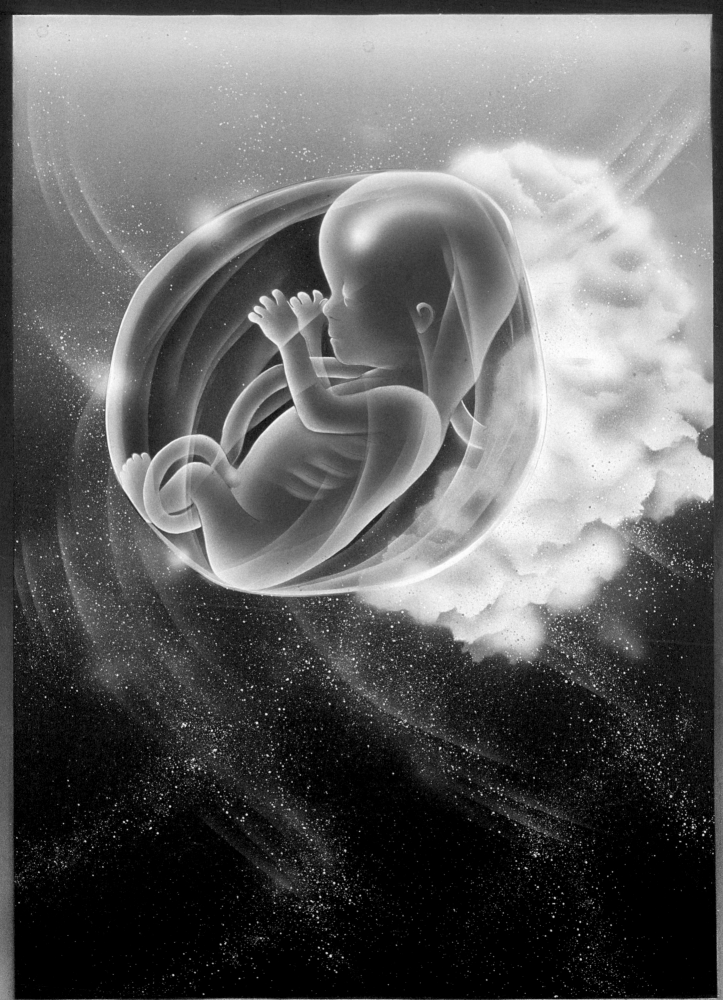

406   Artist: **CAROL GILLOT**   Art Director: Jim Horn   Agency: Botto, Rossner, Horn, Messinger   Client: Armour Pharmaceutical Company

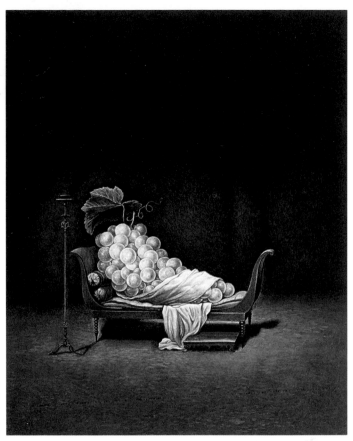

407
Artist: **KINUKO Y. CRAFT**
Art Director: Mylene Turek
Agency: Homer and Durham
Client: Moreau Wines

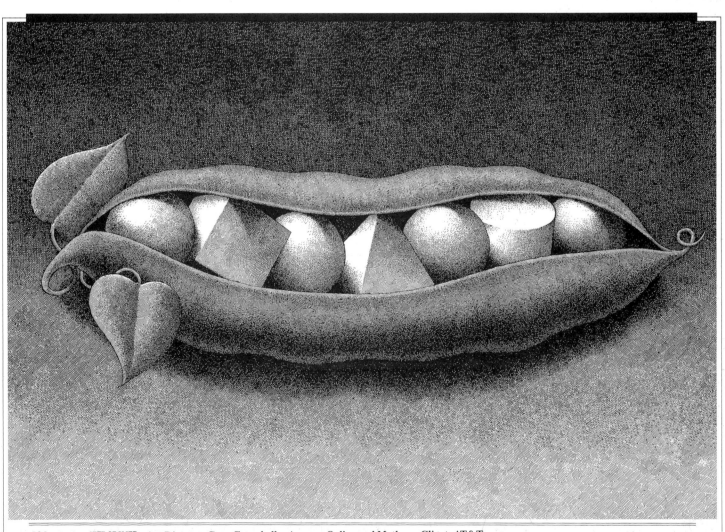

408 Artist: **JEFF SEAVER** Art Director: Greg Campbell Agency: Oglivy and Mather Client: AT&T

409
Artist: **JUDY PEDERSEN**

410
Artist: **KAREN KLUGLEIN**

411 Artist: **KINUKO Y. CRAFT**   Art Director: Mylene Turek   Agency: Homer and Durham   Client: Moreau Wines

412
Artist: **BRALDT BRALDS**
Art Director: Steve Stone
Agency: Ketchum Advertising
Client: Ciba-Geigi

413
Artist: **SCOTT JOHNSTON**
Art Director: Phil Hays
Client: Art Center College of Design

414 Artist: **ETIENNE DELESSERT** Art Director: Rita Marshall Client: D.E.S. Records

415
Artist: **JOYCE KITCHELL**
Art Director: Robyn Kossoff
Agency: Oglivy Mather Direct
Client: American Express/Hyatt Hotels

416
Artist: **KAREN FARYNIAK**
Art Director: Donna Albert
Agency: Ketchum Advertising
Client: Pennsylvania Tours

417 Artist: **FRAN HARDY** Client: Alpine Visual Arts

418 Artist: **RENÉE FAURE** Art Director: Renee Faure Client: Florida National Bank of Jacksonville

419
Artist: **KINUKO Y. CRAFT**
Art Director: Neal Pozner
Client: RCA Records

420 Artist: **MICHAEL GARLAND**

421 Artist: **LINDA HELTON**   Art Director: Ron Sullivan   Agency: Sullivan Perkins   Client: Eldorado

422 Artist: **DOUGLAS SMITH** Art Director: Salvatore Sinare Agency: Foote, Cone & Belding Client: Pacific Telesis

423
Artist: **BRAD HOLLAND**
Art Director: Mark Larson
Client: CBS Records

424
Artist: **STEVE JOHNSON**
Art Director: Melissa Stone
Client: Hazelden Foundation

425 Artist: **PETE MUELLER** Art Directors: Brian Fox / Robert Biro Agency: B.D. Fox & Friends Client: Columbia Pictures

426
Artist: **LUIS CRUZ AZACETA**
Art Director: Joseph Stelmach
Client: RCA Records

427
Artist: **MICHAEL DAVID BROWN**
Art Director: Michael David Brown
Client: Art Litho Company

429
Artist: **MICHAEL DAVID BROWN**
Art Director: Michael David Brown
Client: Art Litho Company

428
Artist: **MICHAEL DAVID BROWN**
Art Director: Michael David Brown
Client: Art Litho Company

430
Artist: **ALAN E. COBER**
Art Director: Morris Sendor
Client: Postermotions

431 Artist: **BARRY E. JACKSON**   Art Director: Greg Clancey   Agency: Chiat Day   Client: Pioneer Stereo

432 Artist: **ROBERT HUNT** Art Director: Dexter Fedor Agency: Eisaman, Johns & Laws Client: Pendleton Wool Mills

433 Artist: **VICTOR JUHASZ** Art Directors: Susan Folton / Art Gilmore Agency: John Emmerling, Inc. Client: Discover

JURY

Braldt Bralds
Chairman
Illustrator

Jeff Seaver
Illustrator

Ronn Campisi
Art Director,
Boston Globe Magazine

Barron Storey
Illustrator

Bernie D'andrea
Illustrator

Richard Warner
Art Director,
Sports Illustrated

John English
Illustrator

Lonni Sue Johnson
Illustrator

AWARD WINNERS

Rafal Olbinski
Gold Medal

Brad Holland
Silver Medal

David Lesh
Silver Medal

Tom Sciacca
Silver Medal

INSTITUTIONAL

434 Artist: **RAFAL OLBINSKI**   Art Director: Rafal Olbinski   Client: Daytop

GOLD MEDAL

435 Artist: **BRAD HOLLAND**   Art Director: Janine Mayhew   Client: Springdale Graphics
SILVER MEDAL

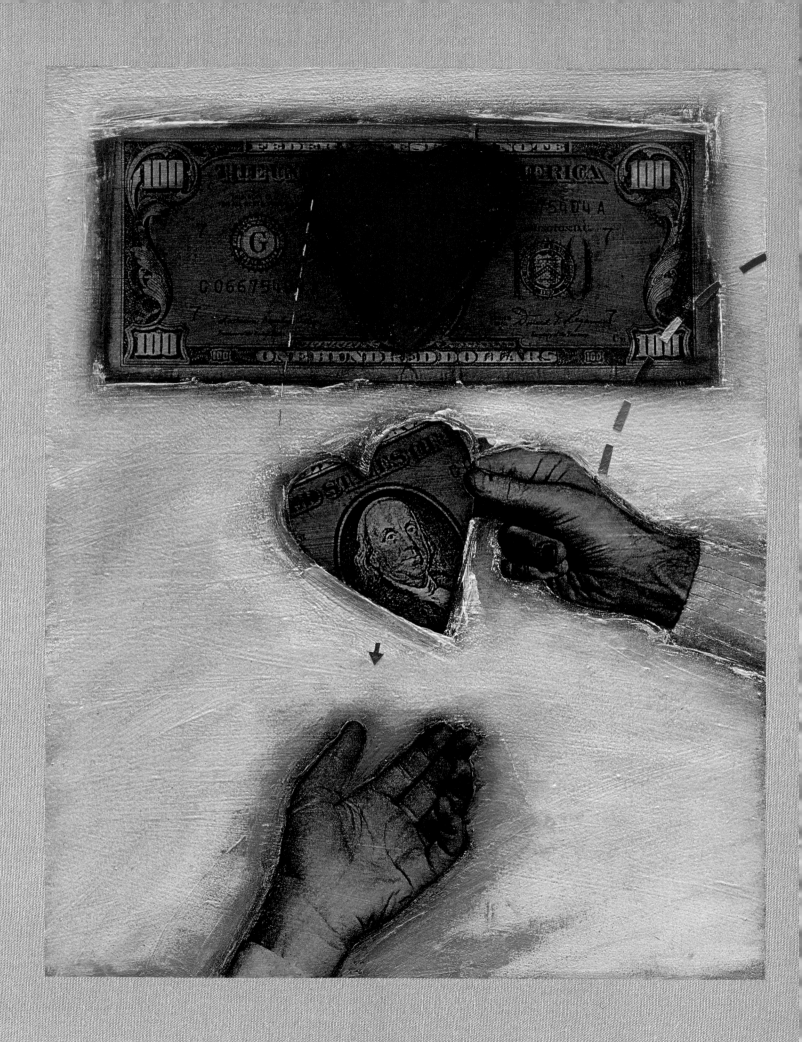

436 Artist: **DAVID LESH** Art Director: Dru De Santis

SILVER MEDAL

437 Artist: **TOM SCIACCA**   Art Director: Tom Sciacca   Client: Michael Esposito/Double Page Gallery

438
Artist: **FRANCIS LIVINGSTON**

439 Artist: **CURT DOTY** Art Director: Clement Mok Client: Apple, Inc.

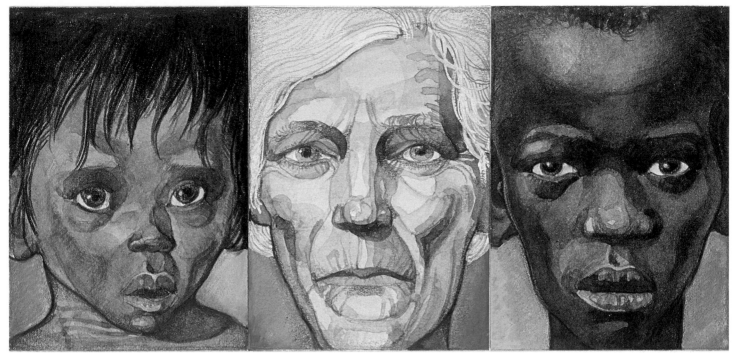

440
Artist: **JERRY PINKNEY**
Art Director: Jack Williams
Client: US Postal Service

441
Artist: **KELLY STRIBLING**
Art Director: Ann Barrington
Client: Neiman Marcus

442 Artist: **MARSHALL ARISMAN**   Art Director: Jim Williams   Client: Advertising and Design Services, Inc.

443
Artist: **LEE EDWARD WOLF**

444 Artist: **JEFFREY J. SMITH** Art Director: Katherine Howell Client: University of Buffalo

445 Artist: **VINCENT NASTA**

446 Artist: **JOANIE SCHWARZ**

447
Artist: **LINDA HELTON**
Art Director: Ron Sullivan
Agency: Sullivan Perkins
Client: Eastfield College

448 Artist: **MARK BRAUGHT**   Art Director: Paula Differding   Client: Art Directors Club of Indiana

449 Artist: **KINUKO Y. CRAFT** Art Director: Bennett Robinson Client: H.J. Heinz Company

450
Artist: **MICHAEL G. COBB / DIANE DELANCEY**
Art Directors: Michael G. Cobb / Diane Delancey
Client: Art Directors Club of Boston

451
Artist: **RANDALL ENOS**

452 Artist: **DAVID SHANNON**   Art Director: Barbara Nieminen   Client: Squibb Corporation

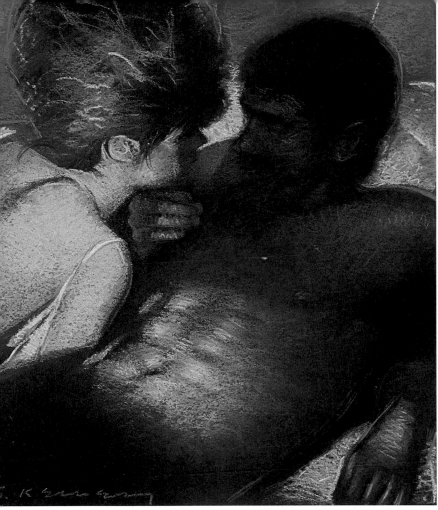

453 Artist: **GARY KELLEY** Art Director: Gary Kelley Client: Hellman Associates

454
Artist: **PETER HALL**
Art Director: Susan Snitzer
Client: Rhode Island Council of Community Mental Health Centers

455
Artist: **GREG HARGREAVES**
Art Director: Tony Luetkehans
Client: Hellman Associates

456 Artist: **KENT WILLIAMS**

457
Artist: **DENIS PARKHURST**
Art Directors: Ken Parkhurst / Inju Sturgeon
Client: UCLA Extension Department

459 Artist: **CELIA CURRY**   Art Director: Celia Curry   Client: Full Circle Cards

460
Artist: **MILTON GLASER**
Art Director: Milton Glaser
Client: International Association of Cooking Professionals

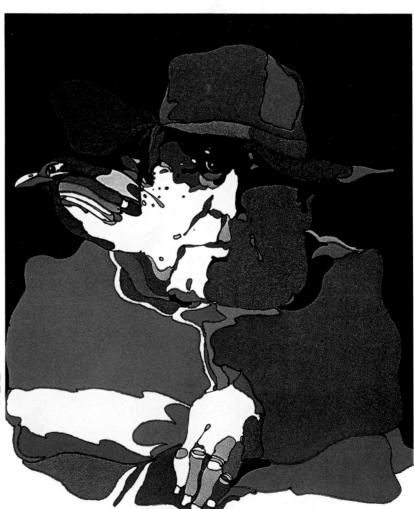

461
Artist: **MICHAEL DAVID BROWN**
Art Director: Michael David Brown
Client: Colorcraft Litho, Inc.

462 Artist: **JOEL SPECTOR**

463 Artist: **MALCOLM T. LIEPKE**

464 Artist: **JAMES McMULLAN**   Art Director: Bennett Robinson   Client: H.J. Heinz Company

465 Artist: **WILSON McLEAN**   Art Director: Kate Mackie   Client: Edinburgh Festival

466
Artist: **PAUL ORLANDO**
Art Director: Nancy Kreinheder
Client: New Holland

467
Artist: **PAUL ORLANDO**
Art Director: Nancy Kreinheder
Client: New Holland

468 Artist: **JOHN RUSH** Art Director: David Bartels Agency: Bartels and Carstens Client: Anheuser-Busch

469
Artist: **RAFAL OLBINSKI**
Art Directors: Nigel Holmes / Rafal Olbinski
Client: APM

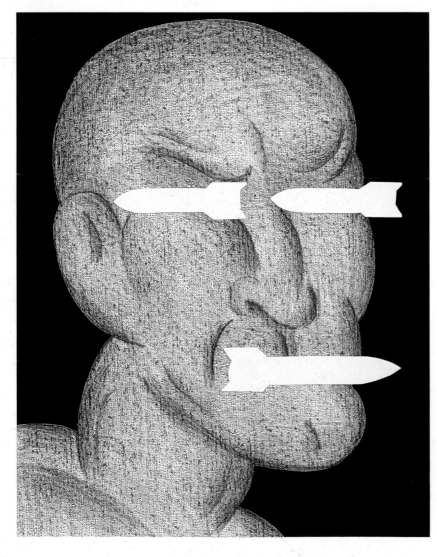

470
Artist: **SEYMOUR CHWAST**
Art Director: Seymour Chwast
Client: The Shoshin Society

471 Artist: **ROBERT FORSBACH**   Art Director: Robin Ayres   Agency: Richards Brock Miller Mitchell   Client: March of Dimes

472 Artist: **ROBERT FORSBACH**   Art Director: Robin Ayres   Agency: Richards Brock Miller Mitchell   Client: March of Dimes

473
Artist: **ETIENNE DELESSERT**
Art Director: Etienne Delessert
Client: Supersaxo-Carabosse

474 Artist: **T.E. BREITENBACH**

475
Artist: **RICK KRONINGER**
Art Director: Cheri Groom
Agency: Atkins Advertising
Client: San Antonio Convention and Visitors Bureau

476
Artist: **REGAN DUNNICK**
Art Director: Shinichiro Tora
Client: Hotel Barmen's Association

477
Artist: **MICHAEL SCHWAB**
Art Director: Bill West
Agency: Taylor / Alexander, Inc.
Client: Clarke Graphics

478
Artist: **BOB PETERS**
Art Director: Ann Hubbard
Client: Arizona Portfolio

479
Artist: **PAUL CALLE**
Art Director: Ellen Pedersen
Client: Mill Pond Press

480 Artist: **MARK BRAUGHT** Art Director: Katie Kennedy Client: Ball State University

481   Artist: **GUY BILLOUT**   Art Director: Robert Miles Runyan   Client: Micom Systems, Inc.

482
Artist: **BART FORBES**
Art Director: Janet Blank
Client: Mead Paper Company

483 Artist: **DOUG JOHNSON** Art Director: Peter Morance Agency: McCaffrey & McCall, Inc. Client: Mercedes-Benz

485
Artist: **MARK MCMAHON**
Art Director: Beth Doddle
Client: De Paul University

487
Artist: **STEVEN GUARNACCIA**
Art Director: Susan Hochbaum
Client: University of Wisconsin

486
Artist: **STEVEN GUARNACCIA**
Art Director: Louise Fili
Client: Pantheon Books

488 Artist: **JAN PERKINS**

489
Artist: **JOE DUFFY**
Art Director: Joe Duffy
Client: Fallon McElligott

490 Artist: **GEORGE MASI**

491 Artist: **PETER M. FIORE**

492 Artist: **GERRY GERSTEN** Art Director: Paul Hagan Agency: W.B. Donner & Co. Client: Pratt Library

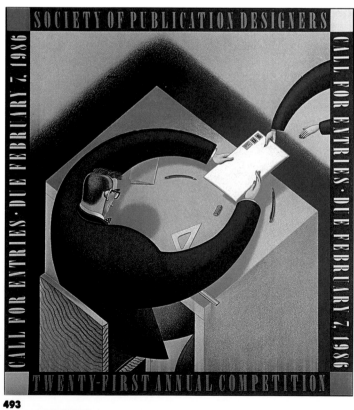

493
Artist: **DAVE CALVER**
Art Directors: Melissa Tardiff / Michael Grossman
Client: Society of Publication Designers

494
Artist: **BOB CONGE**
Art Director: Bob Conge
Client: Park Avenue Merchants Association

495 Artist: **MARK HESS**   Art Director: Kevin Kuester   Client: First Bank of Minnesota

496 Artist: **LARRY A. GERBER**

497 Artist: **RAFAL OLBINSKI**   Art Director: Rafal Olbinski   Client: Polish American Artists Socie

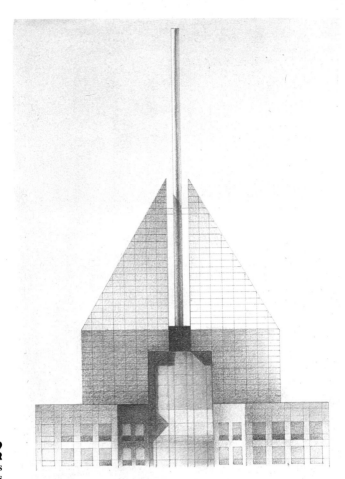

499
Artist: **ANDY DEARWATER**
Art Director: Lowell Williams
Client: Hillman Properties

500
Artist: **JAMES RIZZI**
Art Director: Susan Skoorka
Client: Queens Council on the Arts

498
Artist: **TOM BUCHS**
Client: Art Factory

501
Artist: **TOM McNEFF**
Art Director: Jerry Herring
Agency: Herring Design

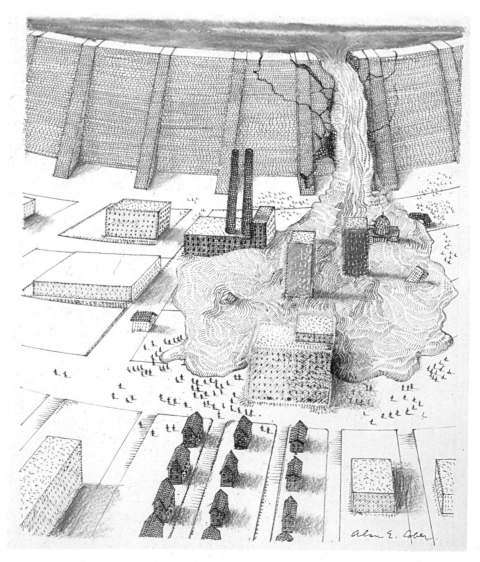

502
Artist: **ALAN E. COBER**
Art Director: Amy Knoell
Client: American International Group

504 Artist: **ROBERT M. CUNNINGHAM** Art Director: Bennett Robinson Client: Continental Corporation

505
Artist: **ALLEN GARNS**
Art Director: David Page
Client: Samaritan Health Services

506
Artist: **MORGAN PICKARD**
Art Director: Ken Kulwiek
Client: Thomas Relth and Company, Inc.

507 Artist: **WENDELL MINOR** Art Director: Janine Mayhew Client: Springdale Graphics

508 Artist: **RICHARD WEHRMAN**　Art Director: Richard Wehrman　Client: Bob Wright Creative Group

509 Artist: **DONALD G. JONES**

510
Artist: **STEVE SHOCK**
Art Director: Steve Shock
Client: Hellman Associates

511 Artist: **MARK HESS** Art Director: Kevin Kuester Client: First Bank of Minnesota

512
Artist: **BOB CONGE**
Art Director: Bob Conge
Client: Marketing Communicators of Rochester

513
Artist: **EDWARD SOREL**
Art Director: Edward Sorel
Client: New School of Social Research

514   Artist: **EDWARD SOREL**   Art Director: Everett Halvorsen   Client: Forbes

515 Artist: **JERRY MORIARTY** Art Director: Bill Kobasz Client: School of Visual Arts

Artist: **BRUCE STRACHAN**

517 Artist: **ROBERT NEUBECKER**   Art Director: Jennifer Napoli   Client: W.B.M.G. Associates

519
Artist: **REGAN DUNNICK**
Art Director: Shelby McDuff
Client: Carpet Resources

518
Artist: **ALLEN GARNS**
Art Director: Ted Nuttall
Client: PSMC

521
Artist: **ED LINDLOF**
Art Director: Peggy Tomarkin
Agency: D'Arcy Direct
Client: Banquet Foods / Light & Elegant

522
Artist: **FRANCES JETTER**
Art Directors: David Barnett / Dennis Barnett
Client: AIG (American International)

20
Artist: **BRYAN LEISTER**
Art Director: Caesar Jackson
Client: U.S. Government

523
Artist: **KATHERINE MAHONEY**
Art Director: Pat Robinson
Agency: Cipriani Associates
Client: Honeywell

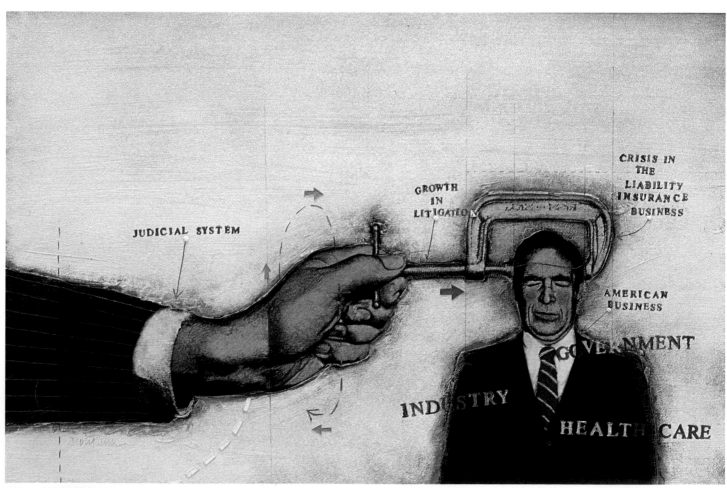

524 Artist: **DAVID LESH** Client: Peat Marwick

525 Artist: **SALVADOR BRU** Art Director: Ethel Kessler Client: Hiroshima 40th Anniversa

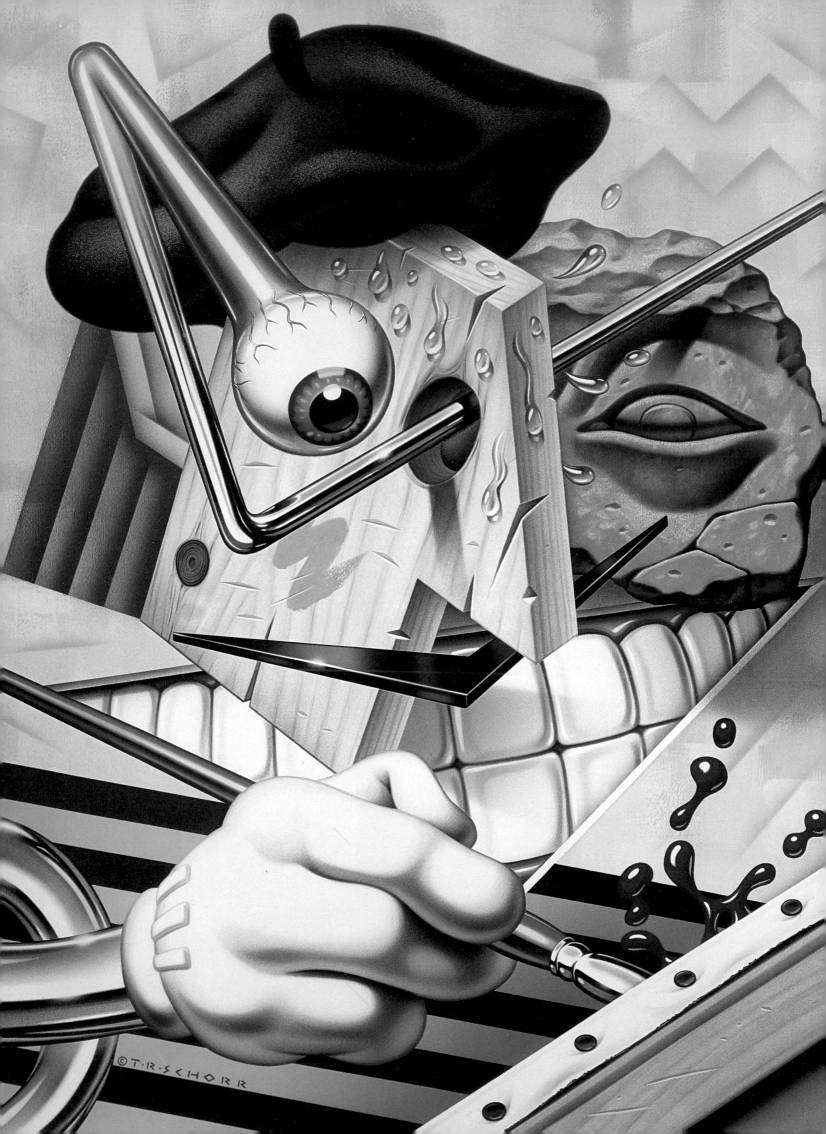

527
Artist: **MARK ENGLISH**
Art Director: Bob Paige
Agency: Paige Group
Client: Mohawk Paper

528
Artist: **MARK ENGLISH**
Art Director: John Creel
Agency: John Creel Associates
Client: Ski

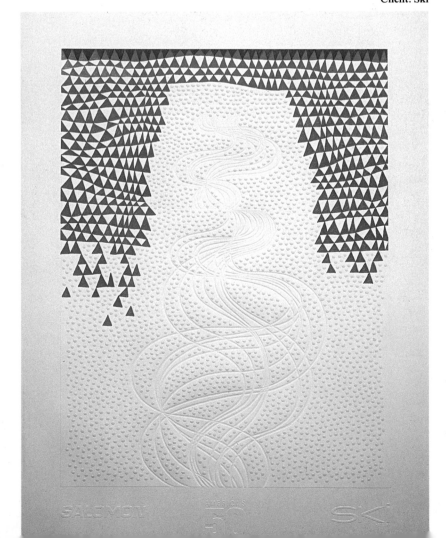

526
Artist: **TODD SCHORR**
Art Director: Todd Schorr
Client: Print Magazine

529 Artist: **DAVID LESH** Art Director: Frank Lionetti Client: Waldenbooks

531
Artist: **LIZ KATHMAN GRUBOW**
Art Director: Liz Kathman Grubow
Client: Cincinnati Symphony Orchestra

530
Artist: **DAVID LESH**
Art Director: Jamie Feldman
Client: Federal Reserve Bank of Cleveland

532
Artist: **LIZ KATHMAN GRUBOW**
Art Director: Liz Kathman Grubow
Client: Cincinnati Pops Orchestra

533 Artist: **GARY KELLEY**   Art Director: David Bartels   Agency: Bartels and Carstens   Client: St. Louis Union Station

534 Artist: **TERRY WIDENER**   Art Director: Phillip Lamb   Client: Coca-Cola

535 Artist: **ALAN E. COBER**   Art Director: Amy Knoell   Client: American International Group

536
Artist: **FRANCES JETTER**

537
Artist: **DON WELLER**
Art Directors: Ken White / Lisa Levin Pogue
Client: First Interstate Bank

538
Artist: **TOM KEOUGH**

539
Artist: **CRAIG TENNANT**

540
Artist: **KEN GOLDAMMER**
Art Director: John Siebert
Client: Illinois Restaurant Association

541
Artist: **JUDY PEDERSEN**

54
Artist: **THEO RUDNA**
Art Director: Vern Edward
Agency: Wilson, Horn, McClellend and Gra
Client: Georgia Powe

543 Artist: **MILTON GLASER**   Art Director: Milton Glaser   Client: American Association of Homes for the Aging

544
Artist: **DANIEL PELAVIN**
Art Director: Keith Sheridan
Client: The Santa Fe Opera

545 Artist: **GUY BILLOUT** Art Director: Robert Miles Runyan Client: Micom Systems, Inc.

546 Artist: **BALAZS SZABO** Client: Exit Corp, Hawaii

547
Artist: **CATHY BARANCIK**
Art Director: Karl Bornstein
Client: Mirage Editions

548
Artist: **ALLEN GARNS**
Art Director: Janet Taylor

550
Artist: **MELANIE ROHER**

551
Artist: **MIKE HODGES**
Art Director: John Cooper
Client: Fort Worth Society of Creative Communications

552   Artist: **DENISE CHAPMAN**

553 Artist: **BONNIE TIMMONS**   Art Director: Elaine Shiramizu   Client: Shiramizu Design

554 Artist: **EVERETT PECK**

555
Artist: **ALAN E. COBER**
Art Directors: Suzanne Smith / Gorden Fisher
Client: Curwood

556
Artist: **CHARLES SPENCER ANDERSON**
Art Director: Charles Spencer Anderson
Client: Prince Foods Canning Division

557
Artist: **JOHN D. DAWSON**
Art Director: Ernie Tasaki
Client: Ortho Books

558 Artist: **CHARLES SANTORE**   Art Director: Jim Jarrett   Agency: Creative Department, Inc.   Client: DuPont

559 Artist: **RICKARD NASS**   Art Director: Rickard Nass   Client: Upper Room Ministry

560 Artist: **ROBERT GOLDSTROM** Art Director: Leslie Morris Client: AT&T / Bell Labs

561 Artist: **CHARLES SANTORE** Art Director: Jim Jarrett Agency: Creative Department, Inc. Client: DuPont

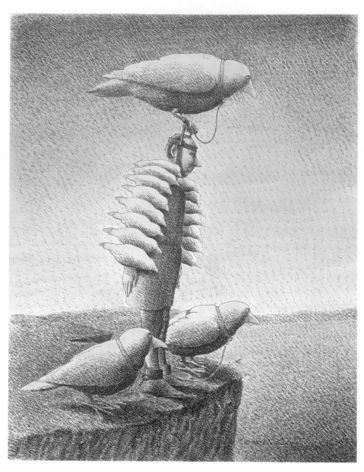

562
Artist: **FRED HILLIARD**
Art Director: Janet De Donato
Agency: Spangler and Associates
Client: Boeing

563 Artist: **GUY PORFIRIO**

564
Artist: **JAMES MCMULLAN**
Art Director: John Clark
Client: Gant Corporation

565
Artist: **LINDA SCHARF**

566
Artist: **BRALDT BRALDS**
Art Directors: Ucho Carvalecho / Ricardo Van Steen
Agency: C.V.S. Comunicaciones
Client: Pirelli

569
Artist: **MARVIN MATTELSON**
Art Director: Sam Howard
Client: Scientific American

568
Artist: **PAMELA J. GLICK**
Art Director: Pat Sloan
Client: Panther Boys Club

570 Artist: **DEBORAH HAEFFELE** Agency: Sand Communications, Inc.

7
rtist: **THEO RUDNAK**
rt Director: Doug Vachon
gency: Vachon Design
ient: City of Atlanta

571 Artist: **JOHN SANDFORD**   Art Director: Anne Boyle   Client: Lincoln Park Zoo

572
Artist: **JOSE ORTEGA**
Art Directors: Bill Kobasz / Richard Wilde
Client: School of Visual Arts

573
Artist: **PAUL ORLANDO**
Art Director: Nancy Kreinheder
Client: New Holland

GIESEKE

574 Artist: **TOM GIESEKE**   Art Director: Robert M. Fitch   Client: Paper Moon Graphics

SOCIETY OF ILLUSTRATORS MUSEUM OF AMERICAN ILLUSTRATION

EXHIBITIONS SEPTEMBER 1986 - SEPTEMBER 1987

AMERICAN BEAUTY

A look at how illustrators have interpreted the typical American beauty—from the Gibson and Christy girls to Brooke Shield's Breck shampoo ad. Over 60 artists were represented.

THE ART OF MEDICINE

A major exhibition of illustrative art for the pharmaceutical and medical industries. Important historical works by anatomical artists Frank Netter, Robert Thom and others, and contemporary medical art as a "Tour of the Body." Advertising and promotional art was also included.

HUMOR '87

Produced by Madison Square Press and sponsored by the Society, this was a juried show of the best and wittiest in gag cartoons, syndicated strips, political cartoons, caricatures, comic book art and humorous illustration. All works were reproduced in a hard cover book, *Humor.*

PAPERBACK—THE FOUR BY SEVEN IMAGE

Over 100 of the best examples of contemporary paperback art as selected by the art directors themselves. All of the major imprints were represented. Printed covers as well as original art were displayed.

PERMANENT COLLECTION: PURCHASE FUNDS AND MAJOR DONORS

Selections from the Society's Permanent Collection acquired with funds provided by our patrons and major donations. Artists included: Edwin Austin Abbey, Dean Cornwell, John Clymer, James Montgomery Flagg, John Held, Jr., Rockwell Kent, J.C. Leyendecker, Saul Tepper, and many others.

THE ROBERT GEISSMANN MEMORIAL INVITATIONAL EXHIBITION: BRAD HOLLAND

The first in what will be an on-going series of shows of the work of non-members. Over 75 of Mr. Holland's paintings and drawings spanning the last 15 years of his career.

An exhibition of the illustration, design, and the life of Robert Geissmann, for whom this invitational exhibition is named, ran concurrently.

SAUL TEPPER & MEAD SCHAEFFER

Carrying on the Pyle tradition of swashbuckling romantic costume story illustration were Saul Tepper and Mead Schaeffer. On exhibit were some of the fine examples of these bravuro painters, both members of the Hall of Fame.

U.S. AIR FORCE ART PROGRAM

Works by Society members painted on location at major Air Force installations. These works have been donated to the Air Force collection.

CAROL WALD

A one-woman show of her recent paintings based on her collages. Preliminary drawings and sketches were included.

HOWARD KOSLOW—AMERICAN MILITARY HEROES

Over 90 original works commissioned by Unicover Corporation for philatelic promotion as First Day Postal issue.

THE ANNUAL STUDENT SCHOLARSHIP COMPETITION

The work of college-level art students from schools throughout the U.S. selected by a panel of professional illustrators. Over $50,000 in cash grants was awarded to the students and their institutions. Over 150 works. This was the 25th Anniversary of this educational event.

THE AMERICAN BEAUTY
ILLUSTRATORS PORTRAY THE AMERICAN BEAUTY FROM THE GIBSON GIRL TO BROOKE SHIELDS
January 7-23, 1987

Beginning at the turn of the century, the illustrator in America has delineated the rapidly changing tastes in feminine beauty in each generation. Decade by decade illustrators fashioned the ultimate in loveliness. At the turn of the century the famous illustrators had their "Girls": Gibson, of course, Howard Chandler Christy, Harrison Fisher, Wladyslaw Benda, Penrhyn Stanlaws, and Coles Phillips' "Fade-Away Girl". James Montgomery Flagg continued the theme in the teens and John Held, Jr. embodied the Jazz Babies of the '20s. In the Depression years McClelland Barclay and Bradshaw Crandall were the leaders in illustrating the beauties of the day. The war brought pin-ups by Petty and Varga, and later in the decade, Jon Whitcomb introduced the All-American Cover Girl. The post-war era was the province of the "boy-girl" illustrators which included Al Parker, Austin Briggs, Coby Whitmore, as well as Whitcomb and a host of others. Though the "boy" was in evidence, the "girl" was the focus of these elegantly designed, romantic works.

Charles Dana Gibson

Coles Phillips

Henry Raleigh, "Lady in Black"

James Montgomery Flagg, "An American Portrait Painter"

J.C. Leyendecker, Easter Cover, *The Saturday Evening Post*

Wladyslav T. Benda, "Healing of the Nations"

Howard Chandler Christy, "Girl Wearing Winged Tiara"

John Held, Jr.

Russell Patterson

John LaGatta, "Three Bathing Beauties"

Haddon Sundblom, "Never Say Die"

Charles Sheldon

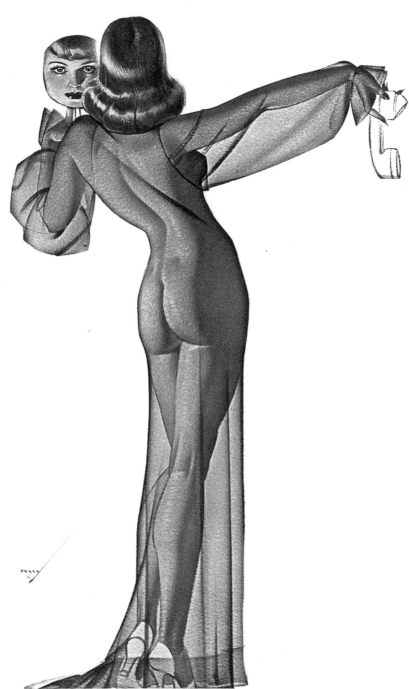

George Petty

Marland Stone, Portrait of Adrienne Ames

John Gannam, "Nude in Front of Mirror"

Jon Whitcomb, "Janet Leigh"

Joe Bowler, "Girl Reaching Out to Man"

THE ART OF MEDICINE EXHIBITION
November 5-26, 1986

Art and medicine have been intertwined since the beginning of civilization. From primitive symbols carved in stone to sophisticated electronic imagery, artists have communicated this special knowledge in a diversity of mediums. They have created anatomical treatises, illustrated medical and surgical procedures and have applied their craft to explain mechanisms and concepts of the body.

Since Hippocrates, the father of medicine, the life of the physician has also been the subject of art. Medical themes have never failed to excite or shock patrons and museum visitors. This exhibition is no exception. There has been no show of comparable scope held in living memory, and the international call-for-entries included the art collections of pharmaceutical companies, medical centers, publishers, NASA, the armed forces, the National Geographic Society, Walt Disney Imagineering, and private lenders. The art spans from the creation of life to the grim reality of death—with even a little humor in between.

Among the many fine artists whose works were included in the exhibition was Frank Netter, M.D., who received the Society of Illustrators Gold Medal "for distinguished achievement in art for medicine."

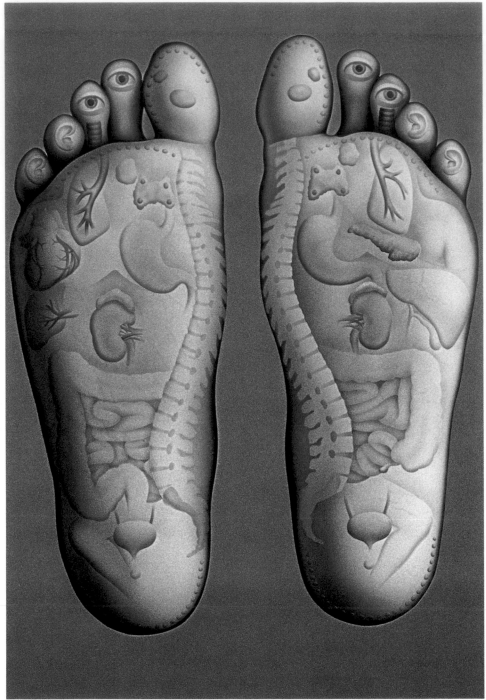

Leonard E. Morgan, "It's Amazing What Some People Think Feet Can Do," Westwood Pharmaceuticals

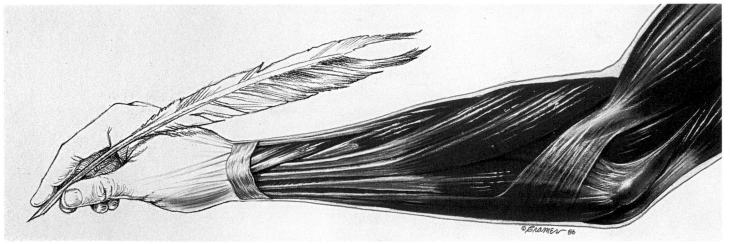

Arthur Lidov, "Neurophysiologist No. 1"

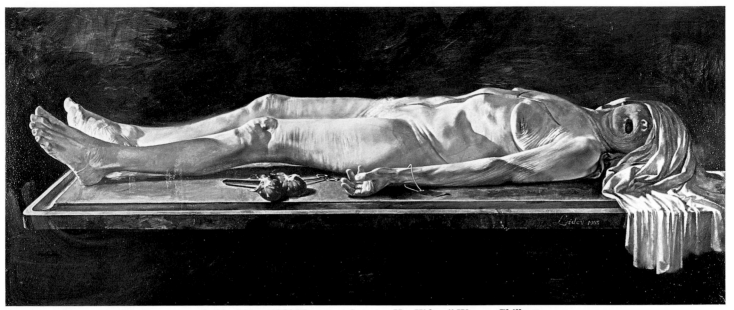

Arthur Lidov, "Old Woman at Autopsy: Her Kidney," Warner Chillcott

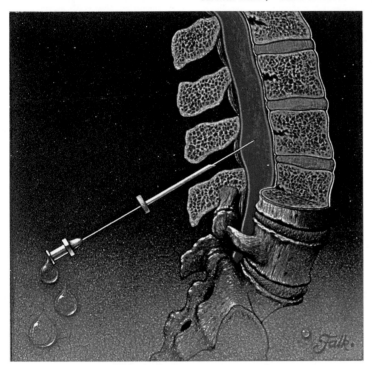

Gustave Falk, "Local/Regional Anesthesia,"
American Academy of Family Physicians

Alex Ross, "Dr. Frank Netter," Medical Times

Donald Kahn, "Urinary Tract"

D.L. Cramer, "Football Player," <u>Natural History Magazine</u>

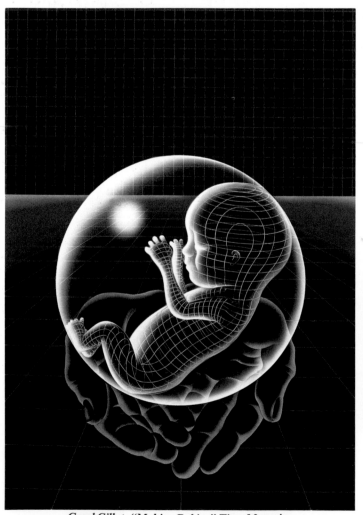

Carol Gillot, "Making Babies," <u>Time Magazine</u>

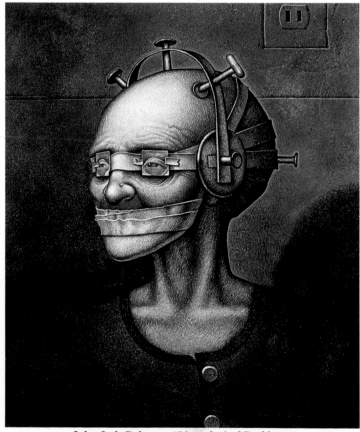

*John Jude Palencar, "Neurological Problems,"
<u>Post Graduate Medicine</u>/McGraw Hill*

Paul Peck, "Inflammation," Merck Sharp & Dohme

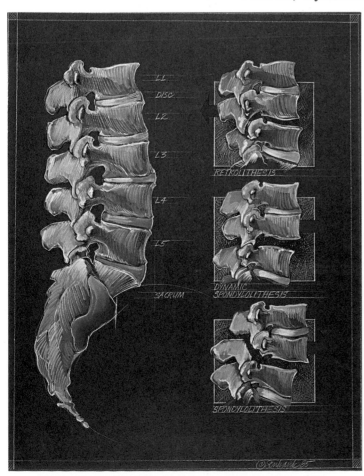

Mickey Senkarik, "Lumbar Spine," Gilbert Meadows, M.D.

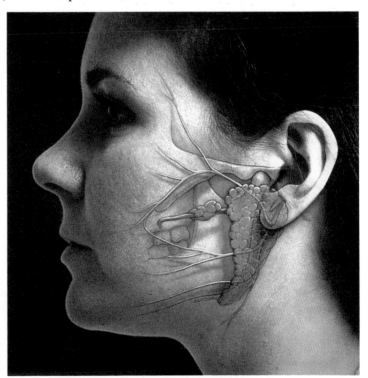

Mark Schornak, "Parotid Gland and Facial Nerve,"
David H. Pashley, D.M.D.

HUMOR '87
September 9-25, 1987

Chosen by a prestigious and very funny jury, Humor '87 contained over 300 of the best of American humorous illustration. It covered all the bases—from subtle mind-teasers and *New Yorker*-style cartoons to pieces with titles like "Crippling gas attacks kept "Big Dave" from enjoying the singles scene," or "Mr. and Mrs. Potato Head pick their noses." Featured were single cartoons, syndicated strips, editorial illustrations, political cartoons, caricatures, comic books, and TV stills. Gold and Silver Funny Bones were presented to twelve award winners.

Sponsored by the Society and produced by Madison Square Press, a book, *Humor*, was published containing a catalogue of the works and an historical introduction by Rick Marschall, who knows everything you ever wanted to know about humorous illustration, and possibly more.

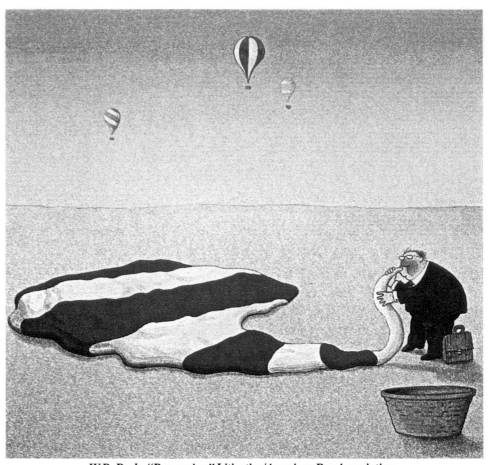

W.B. Park, "Persuasion," <u>Litigation</u>/American Bar Association

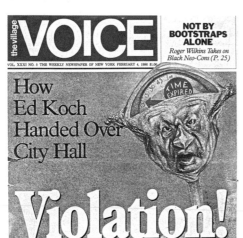

Steve Brodner, "Violation," <u>The Village Voice</u>

Patrick McDonnell, "Have You Noticed?" <u>The New York Times Magazine</u>

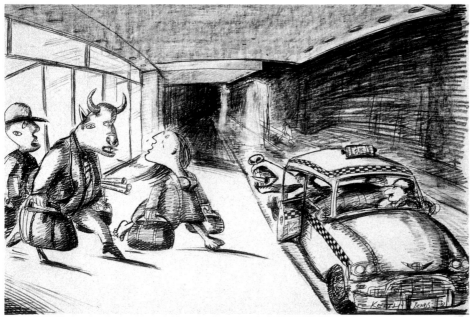

Keith Bendis, "'Guernica' leaves MOMA for Spain,"
Dodd, Mead & Company

Guy Billout, "Phobia," <u>The Atlantic Magazine</u>

Ned Shaw, "New Japanese Diet," <u>Vegetarian Times Magazine</u>

C.F. Payne, <u>Regardie's</u>

Jon C. McIntosh

Peter Sis, "Bachelor in the Kitchen," <u>House & Garden</u>

Dennis Corrigan, "None of us realized that
Uncle Chet was dead at the wheel."

Jeff Leedy, "Façeades of Italy"

PAPERBACK: THE FOUR BY SEVEN IMAGE
July 24 - July 31, 1987

As an area of the illustration industry that has received less attention than it deserves, this exhibition helped to focus on the talents of the best art directors, illustrators, and designers in the business. All selections were made by the art directors from Avon Books, Bantam Books, The Berkley Publishing Group, Daw Books, Dell Publishing, Harlequin Books, New American Library, Pocket Books, Random House, Scholastic Books, Warner Books, and Zebra Books.

With paperback houses commissioning 30 to 70 paintings a month and substantial prices being paid for new titles, the art must be consistent and "spectacular." Many top illustrators were represented in this exhibition and in addition to their original art were the four by seven covers themselves.

Robert McGinnis, Tender is the Storm, Avon Books

Steve Assel, The Last Hard Men, Bantam Books

Pamela Patrick, The Lucky Stiff, Bantam Books

James Gurney, Citizen Phaid, The Berkley Publishing Group

Michael Whelan, Delirium's Mistress, Daw Books

Lisa Falkenstern, The Tender Seed, Warner Books

John Martinez, Duffy, Random House

PERMANENT COLLECTION
PURCHASE FUND AND MAJOR DONORS
December 4-31, 1986

In the belief that American illustration represents not merely a high standard of artistic excellence, but an invaluable mirror of our culture, the Society's Permanent Collection now includes over twelve hundred works by nearly five hundred artists. This is the finest collection of its kind and lists in its possession works by such revered talents as Norman Rockwell, Charles Dana Gibson, N.C. Wyeth, James Montgomery Flagg, Dean Cornwell, and many others. These have come to us through the generosity of the artists or their estates, or through purchases made from the Society of Illustrators Members Purchase Fund and grants given, among others, by the J. Walter Thompson Company. Although works by living artists have always been included, efforts to expand the number of such pieces have increased. In so doing we hope to create a more varied and authentic picture of illustration and to ensure the future of the Collection for generations to come.

Vincent DiFate
Chairman, Permanent Collection Committee

Dean Cornwell, "Tiger, Tiger," 1938, J. Walter Thompson Company Purchase Fund

John Gannam, "Circus Performers," <u>Good Housekeeping</u>, J. Walter Thompson Company Fund

Al Parker, "Palm Court—Plaza Hotel," c.1950, J. Walter Thompson Company Purchase Fund

Mort Kunstler, "Elias Howe Invents the Sewing Machine,"
donated by American Cyanamid Company

Leslie Saalburg, "Family Camping,"
J. Walter Thompson Company Purchase Fund

Guy Arnoux, "le Drapeau de Tontenoy,"
Mr. and Mrs. Elliot Liskin Purchase Fund

John Held, Jr., "Cowboy's Grave," donated by Mrs. John Held, Jr.

BRAD HOLLAND—
THE ROBERT GEISSMANN MEMORIAL INVITATIONAL EXHIBITION
May 20-June 19, 1986

The Society of Illustrators has established a new award to be given specifically to a non-Society member. The artist selected for this first-time honor was Brad Holland, for consistently displaying extraordinary talent throughout his prolific career.

A self-taught artist since he was 13 and a professional since the age of 17, he began publishing in the underground newspapers when he was 24. These ink drawings brought him to the attention of the editors of *The New York Times* Op-Ed page. His art in *Playboy* led to paintings that have appeared in nearly every major U.S. publication, including covers for the *The New*

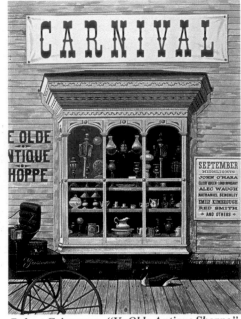

Robert Geissmann, "Ye Olde Antique Shoppe," Coronet Magazine, collection of the Society of Illustrators Museum of American Illustration

Yorker, Time, Newsweek, Life, The Atlantic Monthly, The New York Times Magazine, and others.

Paralleling Holland's standard of excellence was that of the man after whom this award is named. Robert Geissmann, former President of the Society, was a man of great wit and charm. He was a multi-talented illustrator and graphic designer—a born leader and organizer who remains a legend in the hearts and minds of all who knew him. The Society lost a dedicated member and friend upon his death in 1976.

Brad Holland, "Two Good Eggs"

SAUL TEPPER & MEAD SCHAEFFER
September 24-October 31, 1986

The Twenties ushered in the heyday of the swashbuckling romantic costume story and with it developed the talents of two of our greatest illustrators. Carrying on the Pyle tradition, with the added inspiration of Harvey Dunn and Dean Cornwell, were Saul Tepper and Mead Schaeffer. Bold brushstrokes, the use of dynamic pattern, idealized figures, and an overwhelming sense of drama and mood were the hallmarks of these two artists. They brought to their canvases an incredible sense of physical vitality and atmosphere. They sought to convince the viewer and make them "feel" what they were trying to convey. As World War II approached, their subject matter became more prosaic and realistic. Mead painted an armed forces series at this time that helped sell over $132 million worth of Victory Bonds. Saul painted war posters and a series of war messages for the Stetson Hat Company. Many of these were included in the show.

Mead Schaeffer and Saul Tepper have earned a permanent place in the history of American illustration and as this show so aptly demonstrated, a well deserved one.

Bob Crofut

Saul Tepper, "A Captured Knight" for Redbook Magazine, 1934, collection of the Society of Illustrators Museum of American Illustration

Mead Schaeffer, "Bandits Holding Up Coach," collection of the Society of Illustrators Museum of American Illustration

Charles J. Mazoujian, "C-5 Galaxy at Dover AFB, Delaware"

U.S. AIR FORCE ART PROGRAM
September 3-19, 1986

Thirty-five Society of Illustrators members participated in the 1986 Air Force Art Exhibition with fifty-nine works of art on display.

The work included subject matter based on travel to Air Force bases in Korea, Japan, Spain, Germany, Alaska, and many other states in the U.S. In addition, a number of historical pieces were included.

In return for Air Force transportation and hospitality, the artists' time and works of art were donated to the Air Force at a formal presentation in Washinton, D.C., in October. These pieces joined the 6,600 works in this valuable collection of Air Force Art.

Keith Ferris
Chairman, Government Services Committee

Hodges Soileau, "Cooling Off—Volant Rodeo—Pope AFB, North Carolina"

ONE MAN SHOWS

CAROL WALD
September 24-October 17, 1986

Long intrigued with the effects obtainable from placing disparate images side by side, Wald set a precedent with her collage illustrations for which she has received, among other awards, a Gold Medal from the Society's Annual Exhibition. In her one-woman exhibition, titled "Transformations," she explored the uses of provocative juxtapositions to create moods and stir feelings in a series of large paintings based on her collage images.

"Elders"

"Horses and Riders"

"An American Family"

HOWARD KOSLOW–
AMERICAN MILITARY HEROES
December 10-31, 1986

The Unicover Corporation commissioned Howard Koslow to portray 105 outstanding American heroes selected by the Military Historical Advisory Board, chaired by the noted military historian, Major General John W. Houston. Eighty-eight of these paintings, as well as flags and memorabilia, were included in the exhibition. From John Paul Jones to Sergeant Alvin York; from Sam Houston to Audie Murphy; from George Washington to Omar Bradley, these works complemented the U.S. postage stamps that appeared on commemorative covers.

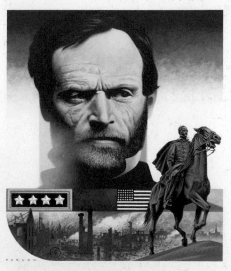

"William T. Sherman-Civil War"
Copyright 1984 Unicover Corporation,
Cheyenne, Wyoming 82008-0001 USA.

"William Halsey, Jr.-WWII"
Copyright 1984 Unicover Corporation,
Cheyenne, Wyoming 82008-0001 USA.

ANNUAL SCHOLARSHIP COMPETITION
April 27-May 15, 1987

The Annual Student Competition and Exhibition this year celebrated its 25th anniversary. The Society wishes to express its gratitude to all those who, throughout the years, have contributed so generously in time and money to make this program the success it is today.

Out of the 4,200 entries which poured in from all parts of the country, 156 illustrations by 132 students were selected for the exhibition, and out of those, 34 received cash awards.

At the Awards Presentation on May 1, 1987, the Society presented $25,000 in prize monies to the award winners. In addition, Hallmark gave full matching grants to the institutions of the award winning students. A special "thank you" to Hallmark for its continued support.

The presentation itself was a night to remember. The students, many accompanied by parents, instructors, and colleagues, were thrilled to have had their work selected. Their beaming faces reflected their appreciation of the Society's efforts on their behalf.

Aside from the Scholarship Competition, the Society has been awarding a Charles Dana Gibson Memorial Scholarship. The first recipient of this honor last year was Eun Ju Kang from Art Center College, who showed such promise that the Committee elected to renew her award for a second year. This year a jury selected the second Gibson Scholar, Chang Park, also from Art Center.

With great pride and anticipation the Society looks forward to the successful future of all these talented youngsters.

Eileen Hedy Schultz
Chairman, Student Scholarship Committee

Samuel Bayer, School of Visual Arts

James Stonebraker, School of Visual Arts

Stephen Johnson, University of Kansas

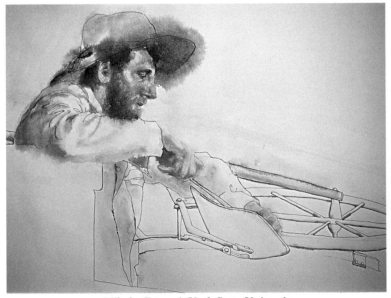

Mihoko Tatsumi, Utah State University

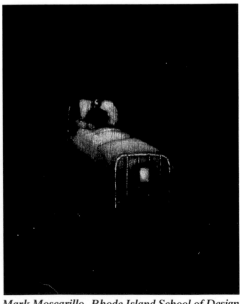

Mark Moscarillo, Rhode Island School of Design

A M E R I C A N · B A L L E T · T H E A T R E

Karen Heyden, Art Center College of Design

Jenny Oppenheimer, Art Center College of Design

John Hom, Milwaukee Institute of Art & Design

Joshua Fallik, Art Students League

Hatton, Enid Vaune
Hawes, Charles M.
Healy, Deborah
Hedin, Donald M.
Heimann, Steven
Heindel, Robert
Hejja, Attila
Helck, Peter
Heller, Ruth
Helzer, James A.
Henderson, David F.
Herald, Robert S.
Herbert, Mrs. James
Herrick, Ira
Hess, Mark
Hick, Mrs. John
Hill, Mrs. Homer
Hill, Sidney
Hines, Jack
Hinojosa, Albino R.
Hodges, Mrs. David
Hofmann, Mrs. Ginnie
Hoie, Claus
Holmgren, Mrs. John
Hooks, Mitchell
Hortens, Walter
Hosaka, Mitsutoshi
Hoskins, Frances
Hosner, William
Hotchkiss, Wesley G.
Huerta, Catherine
Huerta, Gerard
Hunt, Peter F.
Hunt, Robert
Hurst, Mrs. Earl O.
Huyssen, Roger
Ilic, Mirko
Ilsley, Velma
Inouye, Carol
Ishmael, Woodi
Iskowitz, Joel
Jaffee, Allan
James, Bill
Jamison, John
Jankovitz, Frank
Jasper (Tsao), Jacqueline Ann
Jensen, Enola G.
Johnson, Alfred
Johnson, B.E.
Johnson, Cecile
Johnson, Diane Elizabeth
Johnson, Don
Johnson, Doug
Johnson, Evelyne
Johnson, Gordon A.
Johnson, Lewis P.
Johnson, Max D.
Johnston, Don
Jones, George
Jones, Keith Robert
Jones, Robert
Jones, Taylor
Jonson, Jim
Jossel, Marguerite
Juhasz, Victor
Just, Hal
Kadin, Charles B.
Kahn, Harvey
Kalback, Jerry A.
Kaloustian, Rosanne A.
Kamen, Jack

Kamhi, Jack
Kammer, Mrs. William
Karl, Gerald T.
Karlin, Bernard
Kastel, Roger
Katinas, Jr., Charles C.
Kaufman, Joe
Kaufman, Max R.
Kelvin, George V.
Kemper, Bud
Kendrick, Dennis
Kenny, Charlotte
Kent, Albert J.
Kessler, Leonard
Kidd, Steven R.
Kidder, Harvey
Kietz, Alvin
Kimmelman, Phil
King, Gregory N.
King, Jean Callan
King, Mrs. Joseph
King, Mrs. Warren
King, Stanley
Kinstler, Everett Raymond
Kirchoff, Morris A.
Kirk, Mrs. Charles
Kitts, Thomas J.
Klavins, Uldis
Klein, David
Klein, Donald
Klimt, Bill
Koenigsberg, Marvin
Kohfield, Richard
Kohler, Keith
Koslow, Howard
Kossin, Sanford
Kowalski, Raymond A.
Kramer, Dick
Kretschman, Karin
Kristoff, Jeri
Krush, Beth
Krush, Joseph H.
Kubista, John
Kurzweil, Hannah
Kuze, Akiko
Lacano, Frank
Lachowicz, Cheryl
LaGrone, Roy E.
Lamacchia, Frank
Lamarque, Abril
Lander, Jane
Lane, Leslie
Lapham, Robert
Lapick, John
Lapsley, Robert
Larkin, David
Larson, Esther
Laukhuf, Lawrence A.
Lavin, Robert
Law, Polly M.
Lawrence, Lydia
Lazzaro, Victor A.
Lebenson, Richard A.
Lee, Bill
Lee, Jared
Lee, Nan Roberts
Lee, Robert J.
Lee, Tom
Lee, Warren E.
Leggett, Mrs. Barbara
Leifer, Martin
Leone, Leonard P.
Lesh, David
Lettick, Mrs. Birney

Levy, Frank
Lewin, Robert L.
Light, Eugene
Lika, Arthur
Linkhorn, Forbes
Lisieski, Peter A.
Liskin, Mrs. Joyce
Lively, Alton L.
Livingston, Mrs. Robert C.
Llewellyn, Mrs. William
Locke, Nonnie
Lockwood, Mrs. Richard C.
Long, Charles A.
Longtemps, Kenneth
Loomis, Henry R.
Lopker, Mrs. Virginia
Lorenz, Albert
Lott, George
Lotta, Tom
Lovell, Tom
Lowry, Alfred
Lubey, Richard
Lucas, Robert O.
Lunde, Thomas
Lupo, Dom
Lustig, Loretta E..
Lutz, William J.
Luzak, Dennis
Lyall, Dennis
Lynch, Donald C.
Lyons, Ellen G.
Lyster (Armstron), Susan
Macaulay, Mary
MacDonald, John D.
MacFayden, Cornelia
Machat, Michael
Magagna, Anna Marie
Makris, Nancy L.
Maltese, Constance Mary
Mandel, Bette
Mandel, Saul
Manger, Nina
Mangiat, Jeffrey
Manham, Allan
Maniere, James L.
Mantel, Richard
Marchetti, Louis J.
Marci, Anita
Marcus, Helen
Marinelli, Jack
Marmaras, John S.
Martignette, Jr., Charles G.
Marx, Marcia
Mason, Fred R.
Mathieu, Joe
Mattelson, Marvin
Mattingly, David
Mawicke, Tran
Mayes, Herbert R.
Mayo, Frank
Mays, Maxwell
Mazoujian, Charles J.
McCaffery, Janet
McCall, Robert
McCollum, Rick
McConnell, Gerald
McDaniel, Jerry
McDermott, John R.
McDowell, Lynn Baynon
McEntire, Larry
McGinnis, Robert E.
McIntosh, Jon
McKeown, Gloria
McKissick, Randall

McLean, Wilson
McMahon, Eileen
McMullan, James
McNeely, Tom
McPheeters, Neal
McVicker, Charles
McWilliams, Clyde
Mee, William
Meglin, Nick
Meisel, Ann
Meltzoff, Stanley
Mendelsohn, Michael
Mendez, Toni
Mendola, Joe
Merrill, Abby
Metcalf, Roger K.
Meyer, Gary
Meyer, Jackie M.
Meyer, Susan E.
Meyers, Newton
Milbourn, Pat
Miller, Claudia
Miller, Don
Miller, Phillip
Millington, John
Milne, Jonathan
Minor, Wendell
Minuto, Doreen
Miranda, Michael P.
Mistretta, Andrea
Montebello, Joseph E.
Moodie, John A.
Moreland, Marylee
Morgan, Jacqui
Morgan, Vicki
Morrill, Jr., Richard D.
Morrison, William L.
Moscarello, Robert A.
Moschetti, Frank J.
Moshier, Harry
Moss, Donald F.
Moss, Geoffrey
Moss, Tobias
Mott, Herb
Munce, Howard
Munson, Donald
Murley, Malcolm L.
Murphy, John Cullen
Muth, Donald W.
Mutz, Marie
Myers, Lou
Nagaoka, Shusei
Najaka, Marlies Merk
Nathan, Eunice
Neail, Pamela R.
Neale, Russell
Neglia, Josephine
Neher, Fred
Neibart, Wally
Neill, Mrs. John R.
Nelson, Carrie Boone
Nelson, Craig
Nemirov, Meredith
Nessim, Barbara
Netter, M.D., Frank H.
Newborn, Milton
Newman, Frederick R.
Newman, George
Nichol, Richard J.
Nikosey, Tom
Noda, Ko
Noonan, Julia
Norem, Earl H.
Noring, Soren

North, Russell C.
Notarile, Chris
Oberheide, Heide
Oh, Jeffrey
Olbinski, J. Rafal
Olivere, Raymond L.
Orioles, Agnes
Ortenzi, Regina
Osonitsch, Robert
Osyczka, Bohdan D.
Otnes, Fred
Paces, Zlata
Packer, A. Shore
Paine, Howard
Palmer, Thomas J.
Palulian, Dickran
Parios, Arnold
Park, William B.
Parker, Ed
Parker, Jacques
Parker, Mrs. Al
Parker, Nancy W.
Pasquini, Eric
Paugh, Tom
Paul, Mrs. Ken
Payne, George
Peak, Bob
Pecoraro, Charles
Pecoraro, Patricia
Pedersen, B. Martin
Pedersen, Henry M.
Pennor, Robert Russell
Pepper, Brenda
Pepper, Robert
Percivalle, Roseanne
Pereida, Ralph J.
Perrone, Angelo A.
Pertchik, Harriet
Petro, Joseph V.
Philadelphia Colleges of the Arts
Phillips, Robert
Pike, Jay Scott
Pike, Mrs. Zellah
Pimsler, Alvin J.
Pinkney, Jerry
Pisano, Alfred
Plotkin, Barnett
Polenberg, Myron
Popko, Stan
Popp, Walter
Porter, George
Portner, Richard
Portuesi, Louis
Pozefsky, Carol
Prato, Rodica
Pratt Institute
Prestopino, Robert
Price, Alice
Privitello, Michael
Pohaska, Mrs. Ray
Prusmack, Jon
Purdom, William S.
Putt, Glenna
Pyle, Willis A.
Queyroy, Anny
Quon, Mike
Rabut, Mrs. Paul
Radice, Judi
Raglin, Timothy C.
Rainer, Andrea
Ramsay
Ramus, Mike
Rapp, Gerald M.
Raymond, Frank

Reed, Robert D.
Reed, Roger
Reed, Walt
Reich, Heio W.
Renfro, Ed
Rey, Marilyn
Reynolds, Keith
Reynolds, Scott
Rhode Island School of Design
Richards, Irene D.
Richards, Walter D.
Riley, Mrs. Nicholas
Ringling School of Design
Ritter, Arthur D.
Rixford, Ellen
Robbins, Lisa
Rockmore, Julian A.
Rogers, Howard
Rogers, Warren
Rogoff, Herbert
Roman, Helen
Romary, Jr., Alfred J.
Ronalds, Bill
Ronga, Wendy
Roseman, Mill
Rosenbaum, Harry
Rosier, Lydia
Ross, Alexander
Ross, Barry
Ross, Don
Ross, Gordon
Rossi, Joseph O.
Rossin, Lester
Roth, Arnold
Rothovius, Iska
Rowe, Charles
Rudd, Gregory
Rudenjak, Phyllis
Sacks, Beverly
Sacks, Cal
Sacks, Shelly
Safan, Elane Gutman
Sahni, Tiia Taks
Saks, Robert A.
Sanjulian, Manuel P.
Santore, Charles
Sass, Sidney
Sauber, Rob
Saylor, Steven S.
Schaare, Harry J.
Schallack, Augie
Schelling, George L.
Schleinkoffer, David J.
Schmeck, Heidi L.
Schmelzer, John P.
Schneider, William
Schoenherr, John C.
Schorr, Kathy S.
Schorr, Todd
Schottland, Miriam
Schreck, John
Schulman, Lowell M.
Schulman, Robert
Schultz, Eileen Hedy
Schulz, Mrs. Robert E.
Schwartz, Daniel
Schwarz, Jill K.
Scianna, Cosimo
Scott, John W.
Seaver, Jeff
Seiden, Art
Seidler, Ned M.
Selby, Robert
Semler, Robert C.

Sharpe, James C.
Shaw, Barclay
Shaw, Wm. Theodore
Shealy, George A.
Shearer, Julie E.
Shilstone, Arthur
Shoemaker, Col. Alan
Shook, Euclid
Shore, Robert
Sidebotham, Jack
Siegel, Leo Dink
Silber, Maurice
Silverman, Robert
Simard, Claude
Simon, A. Christopher
Sinagra, Attilio
Skypeck, George L.
Smith, Douglas B.
Smith, Gail Hunter
Smith, Marilyn A.
Smith, Paul R.
Smith, Robert S.
Smith, Stanley
Smith, Stephen
Smollin, Michael J.
Soileau, Hodges
Soldwedel, Kipp
Solie, John Andrew
Solomon, Richard
Sorel, Edward
Sowinski, Walter D.
Spanfeller, James
Spector, Joel
Spiak, Sharon
Spitzmiller, Walter A.
Spohn, Cliff
Spollen, Christopher J.
Stanton, Mindy Phelps
Stasolla, Mario L.
Steadham, Richard
Steadman, Evan T.
Stech, Dave
Steele, Robert
Stein, Harve
Steinbrenner, Karl H.
Sterrett, Jane
Stewart, Arvis L.
Stillerman, Roberta
Stirnweis, Shannon
Stone, David K.
Stone, Sylvia
Storch, Otto
Stretton, Gertrude
Stromberg, Mike
Stuart, Neil
Suh, Jeongin
Sullivan, Suzanne Hughes
Sumichrast, Józef
Swanson, Robert
Sweeney, Brian M.
Taback, Simms
Takahashi, Kyo
Tanabe, Masakazu
Tanen, Norman
Tanenbaum, Robert
Tanner, Bert
Tardiff, Melissa
Tauchert, Herman
Tauss, Herbert
Tauss, Jack
Taylor, Dahl
Teaford, Lee
Teason, William I.
Tennant, Craig

Tennison, James
Tepper, Matthew
Teringo, J. Robert
Terreson, Jeffrey
Theryoung, Richard
Thomas, Maurice
Thompson, Eugene
Thompson, J. Bradbury
Thompson, John
Thompson, Kenneth W.
Thurm, Gail
Thurston, Jack
Tinkelman, Murray
Tommasino, David
Tora, Shinichiro
Townsend, Jr., Lloyd
Troop, Miriam
Trooper, David
Trowbridge, Susan B.
Tsugami, Kyuzo
Unruh, Jack
Usher, David P.
Valla, Victor
Van Buren, Raeburn
Van Rynbach, Iris
Van Zwienen, John
Vanacore, Fred
Vebell, Edward
Vero, Radu
Vetromile, Alfred G.
Vidal, Hahn
Vizbar, Milda
Waine, Stanley R.
Wald, Carol
Walker, Mort
Walker, Norman
Wallberg, Susan M.
Walling, Mrs. Dow
Walton, Thomas E.
Wapner, Raymond M.
Wasserman, Randi
Watts, Mark
Weber, Jessica M.
Weekly, Helen
Weiman, Jon
Weinberg, Harvey L.
Weisman, Jerome
Weiss, Morris S.
Weithas, Arthur
Wende, Phillip
Wenzel, David T.
Wergeles, Ed
Whelan, Michael R.
Whitcomb, Jon
White, James D.
White, Mrs. Bernard
Whitmore, Coburn
Whitney, Richard
Whyte, Andrew C.
Willbright, Frank
Willert, Beth Anne
Williamson, Mel
Willinger, Kurt
Wilson, George D.
Winkler, Roy
Winter, Donald M.
Winter, Thelma
Wise, Thomas M.
Witalis, Rupert
Witt, John
Wohlberg, Helen
Wohlberg, Meg
Wohlsen, Sr., Robert S.
Wolf, Ann

Wolfe, Jean E.
Wong, Kwonk Kay
Wood, Rob
Wooten, Vernon E.
Yohe, Tom G.
Zaino, Carmile S.
Zander, Jack
Ziemienski, Dennis
Ziering, Bob
Zimmerman, Marie
Zinggeler, Jeff
Zuckerman, Paul

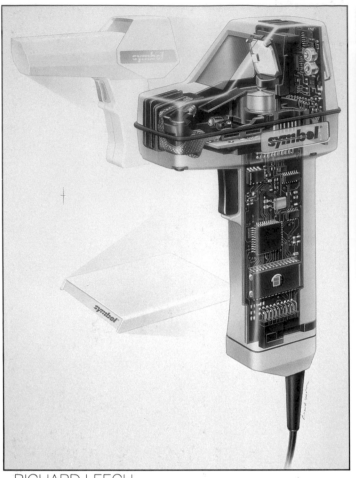

RICHARD LEECH

CHUCK GILLIES *Courtesy of Skidmore Sahratian*

BOB BERRAN

GARRY COLBY

(212) 986-5080

Mendola LTD.

GRAYBAR BLDG · 420 LEXINGTON AVE · SUITE 2911 · NEW YORK, N.Y. 10170

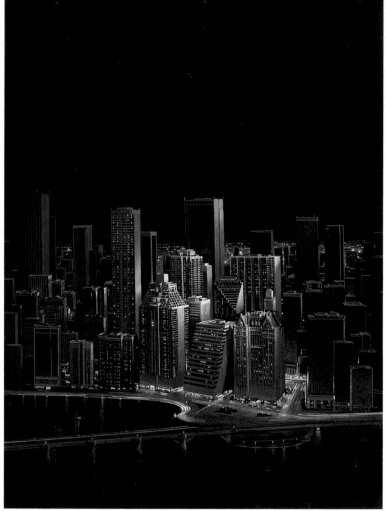

ATTILA HEJJA

DAVE
HENDERSON

LARRY SCHWINGER

JIM CAMPBELL

PETER FIORE

DONNA DIAMOND

PAUL ALEXANDER

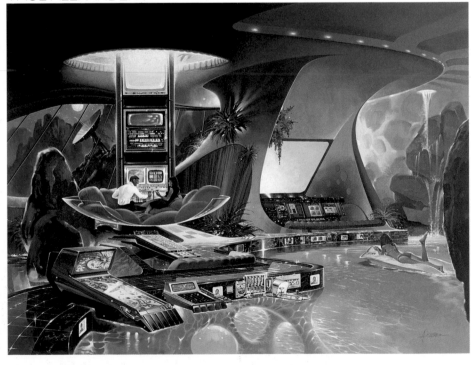

JON ELLIS

JEFFREY LYNCH

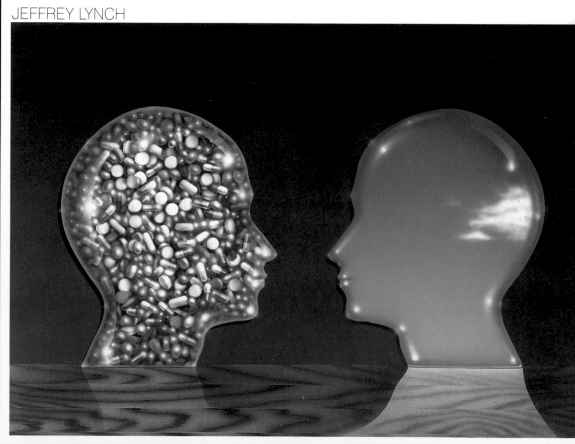

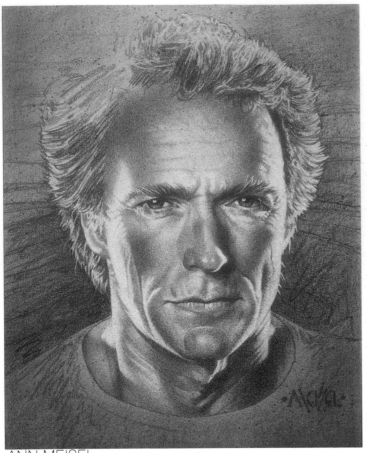

ANN MEISEL

TED MICHENER

JEFFREY TERRESON

BOB JONES

DAVID SCHLEINKOFER

BRIAN SAURIOL

CARL CASSLER

JEFFREY MANGIAT

RAPIDOGRAPH®

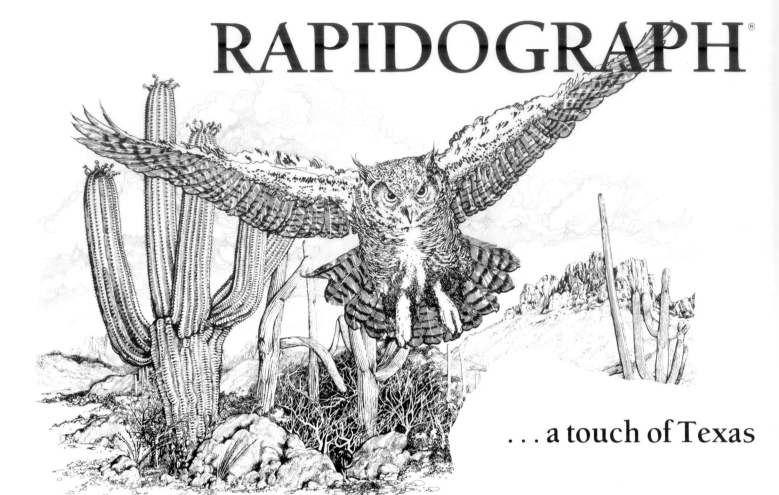

... a touch of Texas

Rapidograph® pen-and-ink drawings are the means by which Raymond S. Wilson expresses the silent desolation in the byways of Texas where life has been lived and passed on for whatever reasons. But by no means, he shows us, are these byways without life. He uses a fine blend of stippling and line to create the silent scene of a predaceous owl or a lonely farmstead patrolled by a mule-eared jackrabbit. Even the weather-abused house, forlorn with the remnants of forgotten occupants, shows life in a vast expanse by the reflection of a hawk and distant butte in a fragment of window glass.

When artist Wilson becomes engrossed in the precise detailing of images in his Rapidograph drawings, he is depending on, but not thinking about the reliability and high-performance value of his Rapidograph pens. It is this dependability that makes the Rapidograph pen the most widely used technical pen among artists, designers, drafters, architects and hobbyists in the United States and Canada. The tubular nib, in 13 line widths, allows movement in any direction on virtually any drawing surface with the ease of, and even less pressure than a pencil. It's easy to develop your own drawing style from one or more of various pen-and-ink techniques, such as stippling, cross-hatching, parallel-lining, scribble-lining, or any combination.

Rapidograph drawings in waterproof ink can be enhanced with colored pencils or pastels, color washes or colored-ink lines using lightfast, waterproof, transparent Rotring Artist Color, or other Koh-I-Noor colored inks.

Along with the 3165 Rapidograph pen, with refillable ink cartridge to facilitate using any preferred ink type or color, Koh-I-Noor also offers the Rotring Rapidograph® pen with disposable ink cartridge. Breathing channels in the Rotring pen do not need cleaning because they are thrown out with the cartridge when ink is depleted, and a new cartridge provides a clean breathing channel; cartridges with black and five colored inks are available. Accept no substitutes for Koh-I-Noor and Rotring Rapidograph pens, the original technical-pen technology.

ART

with Raymond S. Wilson

"Get-acquainted" package No. 3165-BX with a choice of 5 line widths offers special saving with pen/ink combination. Single pens and studio sets in a number of configurations for the self-start, pen-and-ink artist or for gifts. Ask your dealer, or send the coupon for details. Koh-I-Noor Rapidograph, Inc., 100 North St., Bloomsbury, NJ 08804 (201) 479-4124. In Canada: 1815 Meyerside Dr., Mississauga, Ont L5T 1G3 (416) 671-0696.

These drawings by Raymond S. Wilson are copyrighted by the artist and may not be reproduced for any reason without written permission from the artist.

KOH-I-NOOR
RAPIDOGRAPH®
a r**⊙**tring company

Please send complimentary Catalog No. 3 describing Rapidograph technical pens, drawing inks and other artist materials.

☐ Please send names of Koh-I-Noor dealers in my area.

NAME

COMPANY (if the following is a business address)

ADDRESS

CITY   STATE   ZIP

©RAPIDOGRAPH is a Registered Trademark of Koh-I-Noor Rapidograph, Inc.   ©1987

Koh-I-Noor Rapidograph, Inc., 100 North St., Bloomsbury, NJ 08804. In Canada: 1815 Meyerside Dr., Mississauga, Ont. L5T 1G3.

Announcing the first technical pen you don't have to mess around with.

No cleaning. No refilling. No more messy nibs to replace.

Letratech™ is here. And it's everything you ever wanted in a technical pen.

Just take off the cap and Letratech is ready to give you smoother, stronger, more precise line quality. Plus twice the ink capacity of most other technical pens. A unique capillary system that controls ink flow more efficiently and prevents leaking. And a special ink formulation that prevents clogging as well as dry-out, which means 25% greater "cap-off" time.

It also meets all ISO, DIN and U.S. drawing standards for all elements of design and performance.

You'll find the entire line of Letratech pens at your local Letraset Art Materials Dealer. For the name of the dealer nearest you, call 1-800-526-9073.

COMMUNICATION
by Design

Letraset®

Letraset USA 40 Eisenhower Drive
P.O. Box 281 Paramus, NJ 07653-9985

It Takes Masters To Make Masters...

MARSHALL ARISMAN
***LARRY BAKKE**
JOE BOWLER
MILTON CHARLES
BERNIE D'ANDREA
PAUL DAVIS
ROBERT GROSSMAN
RICHARD HARVEY
DOUG JOHNSON
MARVIN MATTELSON
FRANKLIN McMAHON
WILSON McCLEAN
JAMES McMULLEN

JACQUI MORGAN
DON IVAN PUNCHATZ
DAVE PASSALACQUA
REYNOLD RUFFINS
LEE SAVAGE
ISADORE SELTZER
TOM SGOUROS
BARRON STOREY
MURRAY TINKELMAN*
JOHN VARGO*
ROBERT WEAVER
CHUCK WILKENSON
Resident Faculty*

Some of the greatest names in Illustration, what else do they have in common? They have all been summer faculty in Syracuse University's Independent Study Master of Fine Arts in Illustration program.

The Syracuse program is designed for the professional who wants to continue working full time yet improve his skills and earn a degree in a relatively short period. The program is intensive, you'll be challenged, moved out of your rut, and you'll grow, grow, grow. If you'd like to spend a few weeks a year working with some of the top professionals while earning an MFA degree:

call or write
Syracuse University,
(315) 423-3284

Independent Study Degree Programs
Rm 302 Reid Hall, 610 East Fayette St.,
Syracuse, N.Y., 13244-6020

NORMAN	ADAMS
DON	BRAUTIGAM
MICHAEL	DEAS
MICHAEL	DUDASH
MARK	ENGLISH
ROBERT	HEINDEL
STEVE	KARCHIN
DICK	KREPEL
SKIP	LIEPKE
FRED	OTNES
DANIEL	SCHWARTZ
NORMAN	WALKER

REPRESENTED BY:

BILL ERLACHER ARTISTS ASSOCIATES
211 EAST 51 STREET, NEW YORK, N.Y. 10022
(212) 755-1365/6

ASSOCIATES:

NICOLE EDELL
KATHLEEN D'ALOIA

DICK TRACY meets KOH·I·NOOR

DETECTIVE TRACY, WHY ARE YOU LOOKING AT SKETCHES OF CHARACTERS?

LOCHER

BECAUSE ALL GOOD DETECTIVE WORK STARTS OUT WITH SKETCHES OF CHARACTERS...

AND IF DICK LOCHER, WITH HIS ROTRING ARTPEN DIDN'T DRAW US, OR HIS SPECIAL CROOKS- WE'D BE OUT OF A JOB!

Dick Locher, nationally syndicated political cartoonist with the *Chicago Tribune,* has been drawing the "Dick Tracy" comic strip since 1983, and doing it now with a new appreciation for his drawing tools. He is using Rotring's recently introduced ArtPen and ArtPencil to create cartoons, whether for the intrepid sleuth or for editorial pages.

The ArtPen offers a new freedom of motion for ink drawing with your choice of sketching, calligraphy and lettering nibs in a range of line-width sizes. The easy-to-hold, classic styling is designed for the hand, to rest with confidence in a very comfortable no-slip, no-cramp hold. You may choose to use ink cartridges or an optional piston-fill converter for reservoir ink supply.

With the same styling as the ArtPen, the ArtPencil is a real "find" for the pencil artist, or for sketching before inking. All-metal, spring-loaded, clutch mechanism accepts a full range of 2 mm. leads.

Locher uses, as do many of his fellow artists, these compatible companions for the Rotring ArtPen and ArtPencil: Koh-I-Noor's waterproof, non-clogging, dense-black 3085 Ultradraw® Ink; Pelikan Graphic White retouching, opaquing and mixing paint; Pelikan M-20 Gum Eraser with non-crumbling formula and roll-up removal.

Dick Locher is the current creator of "Dick Tracy". He is the natural heir to the perennial policeman, having assisted the strip's originator, Chester Gould, for many years. He has been a staffer on the Chicago Tribune for 15 years. His talents are many, including author, art director, painter, sculptor and inventor.

Distributed by

KOH·I·NOOR
RAPIDOGRAPH®
a rotring company

- Competitive cost
  - Flexibility in production time
    - Knowledge of sales reps
      - Service and fine quality
        - Financial stability

Can you expect all of these from your printer ?

The Society of Illustrators has come to us since its annual book, "Illustrators 23."

 DAI NIPPON is ready to serve you. You can get on the spot consultation from professional salesman.

NEW YORK DNP (AMERICA), INC.
Headquarters
1633 Broadway, 15th Fl.
New York, N.Y. 10019
(212) 397-1880
Graphic Printing Division

SAN FRANCISCO DNP (AMERICA), INC.
San Francisco Office
The Hearst Building
5 Third Street, Suite 400
San Francisco, CA 94103
(415) 788-1618

CHICAGO DNP (AMERICA), INC.
800 Enterprise Drive,
Suite 124
Oak Brook, IL 60521
(312) 571-0150

TOKYO DAI NIPPON PRINTING COMPANY, LTD.
1-1-1 Ichigaya Kagacho, Shinjuku-ku
Tokyo, Japan 162
International Sales Division
(03) 266-3307